THE THEOLOGY
OF TARIQ RAMADAN

THE THEOLOGY
OF TARIQ RAMADAN

A Catholic Perspective

GREGORY BAUM

NOVALIS

© 2009 Novalis Publishing Inc.

Layout: Audrey Wells
Cover design: Ingrid Paulson
Cover image: © Antoine Serra/In Visu/Corbis

Business Offices:

Novalis Publishing Inc.
10 Lower Spadina Avenue, Suite 400
Toronto, Ontario, Canada
M5V 2Z2

Novalis Publishing Inc.
4475 Frontenac Street
Montréal, Québec, Canada
H2H 2S2

Phone: 1-800-387-7164
Fax: 1-800-204-4140
E-mail: books@novalis.ca
www.novalis.ca

Library and Archives Canada Cataloguing in Publication

Baum, Gregory, 1923–
        The theology of Tariq Ramadan : a Catholic perspective / Gregory Baum.

Includes bibliographical references.
ISBN 978-2-89646-079-3

        1. Ramadan, Tariq. 2. Islam–Doctrines. 3. Islam–20th century.
I. Title.

BP80.R343B38 2008   297.2092   C2008-905791-0

Printed in Canada.

We acknowledge the financial support of the Government of Canada through the Book Publishing Industry Development Program (BPIDP) for our publishing activities.

5   4   3   2   1   13   12   11   10   09

Contents

PREFACE

For several years now, Muslim associations in the area of Montreal have tried to become known, establish links with other members of civil society, and adopt a public discourse on responsible citizenship. In these associations, the figure of Gregory Baum has become well known. A renowned theologian, formerly an expert at Vatican Council II, a former professor of religious studies at McGill University, an author devoted to inter-religious dialogue, this solid octogenarian has used every opportunity offered him to be open to others.

Right after the attacks of September 2001, Muslims were the object of a certain "interest." Yet what emerged very quickly from the conversations and reflections of Christians and Muslims in Montreal were elements of a common effort to renew our religious traditions. We were eager to uncover similarities between our understanding of Christian and Muslim teachings and spiritualities, and our interpretation of the history of their respective development. As a witness and active participant in one of the great moments of contem-

porary Catholic history, the *aggiornamento* of 1965, Gregory
Baum became keenly interested in the reform movements
taking place beyond the frontiers of Christianity.

I can bear witness to the fact that this search for con-
tact with the reform tradition in Islam, including that in
the West, is, in Baum's case, expressed through reasoning
imbued with transparency and honesty that are quite rare.
Indeed, his committed research has led him not only to
read the most important works relating to the movement,
such as those of Tariq Ramadan, but also to meet with local
Western Muslims who situate themselves along the same
lines of thought and have attempted over the last decade
or so to interpret their tradition in the context of Quebec
and Canada. Since 2001, Baum has participated in almost
every organized Muslim event, notably those of the network
"Présence musulmane." From the monthly conferences at
various centres and universities in Montreal to the collo-
quia that have welcomed Tariq Ramadan, among others,
as principal speaker, this dean of contemporary Catholic
theology has been present. His attentiveness and his avail-
ability derive from a methodological ethic: always privileg-
ing firsthand knowledge over any other approach.

That is why the book you have in your hands, beyond
being a simple demystification of the phenomenon of Tariq
Ramadan, is also a witness to Baum's deep desire for understanding. He wants to understand the Muslim speakers
who have been inspired by Ramadan in the complexity of
their human multidimensionality. Baum recognizes that it is
impossible to know Western Muslim reformism by passing

over the knowledge of those who carry it forward in the historical context that is theirs.

In fact, the originality of Baum's work is even more significant. If research on the points of connection between reformist theologies in Christianity and Islam have already been the object of many publications, this book is marked by the desire to show that, at the heart of those religious traditions we call "orthodox," theological developments and interpretations are taking place that belong to the high points of religious renewal and the reform movements. The convergence that is the object of Baum's argument is one that brings together in a comparative approach the reformist Catholicism of Vatican II and the reform movement in Islam, specifically the one situated in the West and exemplified by Ramadan.

But then, what is this reformism? The difficulty of responding to this question is as important as the practice of reform itself. Indeed, we are faced here with a methodological option for understanding and applying the foundations of religion in a particular context. It is basically an option located between tradition and modernity. It searches for a balance between the weight of a recognized interpretive tradition and the emergence of an urgent appeal to confront challenges in the here and now.

Catholics and Muslims are often accused of holding fast to their tradition and refusing the rupture demanded by modernity. Challenged to break with the past, we are asked to become "progressive" and learn from the novelty of our time and place. Baum's work demonstrates that this debate is not restricted to one religious tradition. In fact, his effort of comparing the debates in the two traditions reveals the essential point that reform and renewal can be seen in continuity with the substance of the respective Catholic and Muslims traditions.

The great task of any theology that relies on thinking that addresses the present is neither to empty out its heritage in favour of what is new and thrown up by history, nor to tie itself unconditionally to tradition, refusing to create a new jurisprudence and new interpretations of specific circumstances. The essential task is rather to find *the difficult balance between tradition and modernity*, between the heritage of the past and the duty to respond to the present. We must recognize that the most ardently desired effort to renew a school of thought cannot achieve its end without plunging into the soil of its origin. Conversely, the preservation of the religious inheritance cannot hope to obtain a hearing in the present, unless it opens itself and generates creative adjustments.

This is the theological approach proposed by Ramadan in the volumes that best represent his reformist thinking.[1] He offers a reading of Islam that is grounded in its historicity and at the same time actualized by the awareness of its time and place. He links the understanding of the foundational texts and their gloss to a critical knowledge of the present context. He recognizes that dropping the weighty body of sacred texts and approved interpretations would break the bond with the community of women and men who practise Islam in their daily lives. Rather, the interpretation of the scriptural inheritance will have to pass a twofold test, taking into account both the recognized critical commentaries of the past and the pressing challenges of the ever-changing present. Negotiating between text and context, reformist thinking readily moves beyond the scriptural sources by distinguishing what expresses basic principles from what refers to their circumstantial applications.

Reformist thinking can speak positively to the debates regarding Quebec's identity crisis, the norms for reasonable accommodations and the place of religion in the public sphere. Contrary to the perception held by many critics, reformist philosophy allows religion to open itself to dialogue with secular thought and reach out for a universality compatible with modernity. In other words, it aspires to a renewal that respects the principles of *la laïcité*, or secularity. I am convinced that pursuing religion's paradoxical aim of remaining faithful to tradition and open to modernity will make an important contribution to the reconciliation or even the convertibility between the universal and the particular. What we may eventually discover is the reciprocity between the religious and the secular understanding of the world.

This way of thinking obliges us to live religion no longer as a hermetic space or a cloistering protective framework, but instead as an open space of learning, where people become socially responsible, search for points of convergence, are supportive of society's well-being and serve the universal common good – in other words, to acquire the spirit of citizenship.

Committed to this double dimension, women and men firmly established in their religious tradition may become agents of change supported by the broadest of base and affecting the widest audience. Their effort is not to invite people to join a particular project, but rather to have them embrace a way of conceiving society that guarantees the largest amount of shared humanity.

Far from being an abstract utopia, it turns out that this project possesses numerous qualified participants, including Gregory Baum. As a privileged speaker and tireless worker for more than half a century, he is one of those whose history, production and presence give brilliant witness to an exemplary engagement, desire and perseverance.

To Gregory and to all who take up this struggle in their lives, I pay tribute and express my ardent respect.

Salah Basalamah
Damascus
July 25, 2008

A Brief Introduction

After the terrorist attacks of September 11, 2001, the mass media in North America diffused caricatures of Islam and prejudices against Muslims. I was appalled by the shadow of suspicion cast upon millions of innocent people.

As a young theologian I had wrestled against the anti-Jewish prejudice mediated by the Christian Church. I had been invited by Pope John XXIII to work at the Unity Secretariat of the Second Vatican Council (1962–1965). The Secretariat promoted ecumenism and interreligious dialogue and produced the declaration *Nostra aetate*, which condemned anti-Semitism and purged Christian teaching of its anti-Jewish bias.

Now, in the new century, Muslims are suffering discrimination. I am grateful to the Canadian bishops who, in a public statement on October 4, 2001, "deeply deplored the crimes of hate toward mosques or toward Arab people whether Muslim or Christians" and "reaffirmed the respect that Catholics hold toward Islam and its adherents." The bishops remember what the Second Vatican Council said of Islam. Even though Christianity and Islam are different religions,

> the Church regards Muslims with esteem. They adore the one God, living and subsisting in Himself; merciful and all-powerful, the Creator of heaven and earth, who has spoken to humans; they take pains to submit wholeheartedly to His inscrutable decrees, just as Abraham, with whom the faith of Islam is linking itself, submitted to God. ... They value the moral life and worship God especially through prayer, almsgiving and fasting. Since in the course of centuries not a few quarrels and hostilities have arisen between Christians and Muslims, this sacred Synod urges all to forget the past, work sincerely for mutual understanding and ... promote together for the benefit of humankind social justice and moral welfare, as well as peace and freedom. (*Nostra Aetate*, #3)[2]

Since I wanted to do my part to protect the Muslim population against prejudice and discrimination, I began to read contemporary Muslims religious thinkers who wrestled with the problems raised for Islam by the Western Enlightenment and the secular state. I became aware of an extensive religious literature that to me, as a theologian, was enormously interesting, but that was *terra incognita* for most Western intellectuals. Statements of Muslim extremists are faithfully reported by the mass media, yet the scholarly work of Muslim intellectuals attracts little attention. I was greatly stimulated by my attendance at the monthly meetings held by Présence musulmane, a group of francophone Muslims in Montreal who are committed to their faith and to responsible citizenship. On various occasions, this group had invited Tariq Ramadan to give public lectures in Montreal. Once I was invited to share a panel with him. Impressed by his theological effort to make Islam relevant to Muslims living as minorities in the West, I purchased his important books, especially *To Be a European Muslim* and *Western Muslims and the Future of Islam*, and acquainted myself with his religious thought.[3]

It was only afterwards that I found out that Tariq Ramadan is a controversial personality in France. A good acquaintance of mine, the White Father Bernard Tremblay, who uses the Internet to follow the debates about religion in the French press, sent me by e-mail article after article accusing this Muslim theologian, whom I respected, of all sorts of dangerous leanings. I had no choice but to find and read the books published in France that present Ramadan as an untrustworthy Muslim preacher.[4] What amazed me was that none of these books analyzed Ramadan's theological thought. They accuse him of duplicity, of saying one thing to Muslim audiences and another to the secular public; they argue that he persuaded Muslims not to accept the universal republican values, that he is a fundamentalist in disguise, and that, as the grandson of Hassan al-Banna, the founder of the Muslim Brotherhood, he is tainted and possibly dangerous. The accusations against Ramadan and the explanations by which he defended himself are carefully recorded in Aziz Zemouri's *Faut-il faire taire Tariq Ramadan?*[5] This author, not unfriendly to Ramadan, interviews the Muslim theologian, asking him how he reacts to the various accusations made against him in France.[6] Yet even Zemouri is not interested in Ramadan's theological thought – his systematic interpretation of the Quranic revelation. I eagerly bought the most recent *La vérité sur Tariq Ramadan* by Ian Hamel,[7] expecting an analysis of Ramadan's thought, yet I was again disappointed: Hamel deals almost exclusively with the controversial issues raised in France.

What also puzzled me was that Ramadan is not a controversial figure in Britain nor in Canada and Quebec. There he is appreciated as a Muslim thinker who respects human rights and religious pluralism and believes that Muslims can be both faithful to Islam and active citizens of democratic societies. It is worth remembering the significant difference between the French policy of *la laïcité* – a word for which there is no English translation – and the British respect for the role religious communities play in society.[8] *La laïcité* honours religious liberty, yet interprets religion as a purely private matter and thus refuses to recognize its collective manifestation, while in countries of British tradition the respect for religious liberty includes the recognition of the contribution religious communities make to civil society. In Britain, Prime Minister Tony Blair appointed Tariq Ramadan to a government task force on religious pluralism;[9] in Canada, the Muslim theologian has been invited by several public institutions in support of interreligious and intercultural cooperation.[10]

Since no author has presented Ramadan's religious thought, I decided to write this book. This is a bold undertaking because I am not a specialist of the Islamic tradition, I don't know the Arab language, and I am only beginning to acquaint myself with contemporary Muslim religious thought. Still, I bring to the study of Ramadan's theology an attitude that is different from that of his secular critics.

First, I share with Ramadan faith in God, Creator of the Universe. There was a time when Catholics did not recognize that their God was also the God of Islam, yet more recently, following the lead of Vatican Council II, Pope John Paul II has repeatedly confessed that Catholics and Muslims worship the same God.[11] The shared faith allows me to understand and appreciate the theological dimension of Ramadan's work and ask him questions that are of little concern to secular readers. I have discovered in his books that several debates in Islamic thought have their equivalence in Christian theology: for instance, the relation between reason and revelation, human freedom and divine omnipotence, and the will to do good and the divine initiative.

Second, because the Catholic Church first rejected modernity and then wrestled to find a theological approach that allowed a critical openness to modernity, I have great sympathy for a similar wrestling in Islam. I appreciate the theological enterprise of Ramadan and other Muslim thinkers who seek to uncover the relevance of Islam for Muslims living in modern society. There is a certain family likeness between the Catholic and the Muslim theological effort to react creatively to the challenge of modernity. This affinity allows me to read Ramadan's work rather differently then do his secular commentators. I indicate my approach in the title of this book: *The Theology of Tariq Ramadan: A Catholic Perspective.*

While I was writing my book. I had the great pleasure to discover Hans Küng's learned treatise on Islam written from a Catholic perspective.[12] This massive volume is an altogether splendid scholarly achievement that renders an important service to the Christian and post-Christian world.

My book is a modest contribution to Muslim–Christian dialogue. In introducing the reader to the theology of a learned Muslim religious thinker, I offer an interpretation of his thought. I reduce his sophisticated reasoning to ideas and concepts that are easily understood by a Christian reader. This is a risky undertaking, since it does not do justice to the complexity of his thought. An aim of this introduction is to persuade readers to study for themselves Tariq Ramadan's major works: *To Be a European Muslim* and *Western Muslims and the Future of Islam*.

In chapter 1 of this book, I offer a brief account of the dramatic evolution of Catholic theology that allowed the Second Vatican Council to support religious liberty and human rights that had previously been condemned by the magisterium. The subsequent chapters present a theological reading of Ramadan's published work. Chapter 2 reports how he locates his own theological orientation within the entire Islamic tradition. Chapter 3 presents his theology of God, humanity and the universe. Chapter 4 deals with his interpretation of *sharia*, the divinely revealed Islamic way of life. Chapter 5 offers his ideas of what fidelity to Islam means for Western Muslims. Chapter 6 contrasts Ramadan's theology with the theological liberalism advocated by some

Muslim authors. Chapter 7 presents some concluding reflections, including a brief discussion of the controversies surrounding Tariq Ramadan in France. Having studied the heart of his theology, the reader will be able to judge whether the objections raised against him are valid. In my analysis of Ramadan's theology, I have relied exclusively on his published work. I decided not to interview him: I wanted to avoid being told that he says one thing to non-Muslims and another to his Muslim fans.

In the present book I am following the Muslim authors who refer to God as He, written with a capital H, while I normally avoid referring to God by the personal pronoun, he or she. Needless to say, Muslims do not believe that God is male, yet the reference to God in the Quran as He has, as yet, not provoked an extended theological debate. In this book I make use of a few Arab terms that are constantly employed in the Muslim literature that I have read. Here is a list of them:

al-nahda: the renewal movement

fiqh: Islamic law

fitna: the great quarrel

fitra: the natural inclination toward God

hadith: remembered sentences of the Prophet

shura: consultation

ijtihad: interpretation

ulama: jurist, scholar, theologian

umma: the Muslim community

tawhid: the unity and uniqueness of God

1

CATHOLICISM CHALLENGED BY MODERNITY

In this chapter I wish to show, first, that the Catholic Church repudiated the emergence of political liberalism. In the second part, I will analyze the theological reasoning that allowed the Church to respond to modern society in a more creative way. By political modernity I mean the recognition of popular sovereignty, the separation of Church and state, the equality of citizenship, the democratic form of governance, and the defence of human rights, in particular religious liberty. Since the Catholic Church was fully integrated into the feudal-aristocratic order, it strongly opposed the emergence of modern society. It was only in the 1960s, at the Second Vatican Council, that the Catholic Church reconciled itself to political modernity. Because Catholics have had to confront this new political reality for over a century, Catholic theologians read with sympathy and understanding the writings of contemporary Muslim religious thinkers who wrestle with the same issue: trusting in the creativity of Islam, they find in their sacred scriptures support for religious liberty and democratic pluralism.

The papal rejection of modernity

The history of the Catholic Church's resistance to modern society is well known. Soon after the French Revolution and the Declaration of the Rights of Man in 1889, Pope Pius VI condemned the civil liberties in the brief *Quod aliquantum* of 1791. After the revolutionary unrest in 1830s, Gregory XVI published the encyclical *Mirari vos* in 1832, defending the feudal-aristocratic order, ordering Catholics to obey their princes and repudiating, in the name of the common good, the civil liberties, including religious freedom. In 1864, Pius IX published the encyclical *Quanta cura*, accompanied by the famous Syllabus of Errors, vigorously reaffirming the condemnations of popular sovereignty, the liberal state, political democracy, the separation of Church and state, the civil liberties and religious pluralism.

Leo XIII made some hesitant gestures in favour of democratic government. In 1892, he addressed the encyclical *Au milieu des solitudes* to French Catholics, who were monarchists for the greater part, asking them to recognize the republican government of their county as the legitimate authority. He argued that the Catholic Church can live and flourish in any form of government as long as the Church's freedom is respected. Yet when he spelled out the Catholic idea of a just society, as he did, for instance, in his encyclical *Libertas* of 1888, he denounced the separation of Church and state and left no room for democracy, pluralism or human rights. Leo tolerated the approval American Catholics professed for the separation of Church and state in their country, yet when he feared that this exception was being made into a universal principle, he wrote the encyclical *Longinqua* (1895), repudiating as "Americanism" the preference for secular government and religious pluralism. In 1910, Leo's successor, the very conservative Pius X, wrote a letter to the French bishops entitled "Notre charge apostolique." In the letter he condemned le Sillon, a Catholic movement in support of democracy founded by the widely respected Marc Sangier. This is how Pius X summarized the error of le Sillon. "To sum up, this is what its teaching aims at, what it calls the democratic education of the people, namely raising to its maximum the conscience and civic responsibility of every one, from which will result economic and political democracy and the reign of justice, liberty, equality, fraternity."[13]

A sociological interpretation

The papacy's resistance to political modernity is often interpreted as a defence of the feudal-aristocratic social order and of the popes' own religious and secular power. Yet the sociologists of the nineteenth century offered a deeper analysis of this resistance. According to them, the clash between traditional and modern society was more than a political or ideological quarrel; it was in fact a civilizational conflict, a clash between different forms of human self-understanding.[14] The first social thinkers who developed this theme were two French monarchists, declared enemies of the French Revolution: Joseph de Maistre and Louis-Gabriel de Bonald. Their ideas were further explored by social thinkers who were not defenders of the aristocratic order.

While there are differences in the social analyses offered by Alexis de Tocqueville and Émile Durkheim in France, and Ferdinand Toennies and Max Weber in Germany, these sociologists agreed that democratic pluralism and industrial capitalism were creating a new social and cultural world that altered the conditions of human existence, affected people's understanding of the true and the good, and changed their vision of who they were as collectivities. Liberal thinkers in the nineteenth century tended to praise the emerging modernity, looked upon reason as the organ of human liberation, and predicted the progressive humanization of society. Yet sociologists had a more sober view of the new world in the making. They rendered a systematic account of the ambiguity of modern society. While they acknowledged the material and human progress brought about by science, technology, democratic rule and industrial development, they also recognized that modern society dissolved the inherited structures of social solidarity and produced a new individualism, a utilitarian ethic, a spirit of self-promotion and a materialistic culture. Modernity, they argued, opened the door to political and economic policies devoid of any moral reference. Even Karl Marx, who was no friend of the feudal order and its religious inheritance, recognized the cultural upheaval and the decline of ethics produced by bourgeois society. Here is a quotation from the Communist Manifesto (1848):

> The owning class, wherever it has got the upper hand, has put an end to all feudal, patriarchal, idyllic relations. It has pitilessly torn asunder the motley feudal ties that bound

man to his natural superiors, and has left no other nexus between people than naked self-interest, than callous "cash payment" … All that is solid melts into air, all that is holy has been profaned.[15]

I have made this excursion into sociological literature to show that the rejection of modernity on the part of the popes was not simply a stubborn defence of the old order. It expressed the feelings and the fears of ordinary people in the traditional regions of European society who sensed that the modern institutions undermined their culture, their faith and their identity. They recognized the civilizational conflict produced by modernity. The sociological analysis of this cultural upheaval helps us to understand the rejection of Western modernity on the part of non-Western peoples who wish to protect their religious and cultural traditions. Their leaders ask themselves whether alternative models of modernization exist – models of industrialization and political co-responsibility that permit the people to preserve their cultural identity.

The work of the British sociologist David Martin has demonstrated that religion affects the way traditional societies move into modernization.[16] His analysis of the difference between the entry into modernity of Protestant and Catholic countries is very persuasive. Protestant countries have moved into modernization while respecting ecclesiastical pluralism, practising tolerance and relying on the cooperation of various interest groups, be they religious or secular. While these groups disagreed with one another for religious, political or cultural reasons, they all had their own way of legitimating society as a whole. Because Protestantism, with its many churches and internal divisions, has produced a cultural imagination favouring pluralism, the secularization of society did not produce great hostility to religion.

By contrast, Catholicism has produced an imagination that fosters totality. Catholicism presented itself as religion that interprets the whole of life and imprints its character on the whole of society. Catholicism did not provide space for dissent. Dissenters who rejected a single doctrine had to reject the religious system in its entirety, define themselves against the Catholicism they left, and then construct their own total philosophy. Catholicism has accompanied society's entry into modernity with an imagination of totality. This is the reason, David Martin argues, why modernization in Catholic countries has produced a cultural schism between secularists hostile to religion and believers defending the old order.

Martin's analysis is particularly useful for understanding the difference between attitudes toward religion of Great Britain and France. In Britain, secularity is a pragmatic policy to create respect for religious and secular associations in society, while in France *la laïcité* is a secular philosophy that presents itself as the truth. This diversity explains why the attitude toward Muslim associations is so different in Britain and in France. While Martin does not propose his observation as a law – he discusses several historical cases where his thesis does not apply – his analysis may well shed light on the impact of modernity on Muslim societies. Since Islam, like traditional Catholicism, sees itself as a total system, Muslim societies challenged by political modernity have defined themselves either as ideologically secular, as Turkey has done, or as religiously reactionary, as Iran or Saudi Arabia have done. At the same time, Martin recognizes that religions are evolving cultural movements and hence may well learn to adopt a critical openness to modern society. He recognizes that the evolution of Catholicism at the Second Vatican Council has allowed the Catholic Church to become, sociologically speaking, one denomination among others in contemporary society. In Turkey, a spiritual-intellectual current called the Gülen movement – based on the theology of Fethullah Gülen, an important Muslim sage – reconciles the faithful practice of Islam with democratic freedoms and religious pluralism.[17]

The creativity of religion

Some academics, unaware of the creativity of religion, suppose that religions are unchanging systems of ideas and values. I still remember the polemics of Paul Blanshard, who, writing in the 1940s and '50s, argued that Roman Catholicism, hostile to democracy, pluralism and the separation of Church and state, prevented Roman Catholics from becoming trustworthy citizens and constituted a danger to the American Republic.[18] He postulated a clash of civilizations between Protestant and Catholics societies. When I met Mr. Blanshard in Rome during the Vatican Council, he was greatly puzzled and did not know what to say.

Today, Samuel Huntington advocates the theory of the clash of civilizations between Western and Islamic societies.[19] He argues that Western values, which he considers Christian, are incompatible with Muslim values; hence, conflict between these cultural spheres is inevitable. This is an error on three accounts. First, the Western respect for religious pluralism is not an ancient Christian value, as Jews would testify. Second, rereading their sacred texts, religions are able to move forward and redefine their values: Catholics no longer burn heretics, nor are Muslims incapable of respecting religious pluralism. Third, millions of Muslims now live in the West and practise their faith as Westerners. Tariq Ramadan, whose theology I present in this book, was born in Switzerland, was educated in the West and addresses his theology principally to Western Muslims. Huntington fails to recognize that religions, far from being static cultures, are alive by an inner dynamism and hence capable of evolving.

In the nineteenth century, Catholics living as minorities in Protestant or secular societies were embarrassed by the papal repudiation of the principle of religious liberty. They were glad that their society respected religious pluralism and thus allowed them to live in peace and have thriving parishes, even if they suffered some discrimination. Progressive French Catholics were unhappy that tolerance was not a virtue recognized by their Church. Bishop Dupanloup offered them an interpretation of the Syllabus of Errors that allowed them to sidestep the papal teaching. In countries where Catholics constitute the majority, they must demand that the government protect the Catholic Church and restrain heretical and false religions – Dupanloup called this "the thesis." In countries where Catholics constitute a minority, they must support the freedom of religion because in their situation, this serves the Catholic faith – Dupanloup called this "the hypothesis."[20] His proposal became the Church's official stand.

Many Catholics were unhappy with this opportunistic theory, especially Catholics involved in political life in democratic societies. But to change the Church's official teaching required a profound spiritual conversion. A dramatic turn to a critical openness to modernity took place in the life of the Catholic philosopher Jacques Maritain, whose thought was to have a profound influence on the Catholic world, including the papacy.

Shortly after becoming Catholics in 1906, Jacques Maritain and his wife, Raïssa, joined the ultra-conservative movement l'Action française under the leadership of the atheist social thinker Charles Maurras, an enemy of democracy and a defender of the monarchy. In 1921, Maritain published his book *Antimoderne*.[21] When Pius XI condemned l'Action française in 1926, Maritain was deeply shaken. A year later, in 1927, he published *Primauté du spiritual*,[22] in which he revealed his own anguish, analyzed the crisis within the French Church, defended the Pope's teaching authority, and pleaded with Catholics to accept the recent condemnation. He argued that l'Action française had been condemned not because of its conservative resistance to political liberalism, but because Charles Maurras, as a professed atheist, was not a suitable leader for a Catholic movement. Maritain tried to console his Catholic readers by insisting on the abiding truth of the Syllabus of Errors and other papal documents condemning the false ideas of liberalism, such as popular sovereignty, parliamentary democracy, the value-neutral state, and the superiority of personal freedom over truth and justice.[23] Still, in this little book, Maritain also suggested that to overcome the errors of modernity, Catholics should return to the sources of their faith and move forward in a new and original way.

Maritain's next book, *Du régime temporel et de la liberté*,[24] published in 1933, offers two new ideas. First, drawing upon the Aristotelian-Thomistic tradition, Maritain presents philosophical reasons for human freedom and human self-responsibility. Gifted with intelligence, moral consciousness and free will, people are never simply subjects of a temporal regime. They always transcend the regime as responsible agents. Human freedom is the power to discern moral truth as an objective order and to do what is good. Maritain here offers a metaphysical foundation of human rights that is quite different from the utilitarian arguments proposed by classical liberal theory.

In the same book, Maritain also makes a distinction between two different historical contexts in which the Church exercises its pastoral ministry: the sacred order of medieval and baroque society, and the profane order of modern society marked by a pluralism of truth and values. Long before it was widely acknowledged, Maritain recognized the end of Christendom and the arrival of a secular age in which the Church was offered no privileges. He now argued that the Church's conservative social teaching (the rejection of democracy and religious liberty) was appropriate in the order of Christendom, yet as the Church moves into the secular order of the present, this teaching must be rethought and reformulated.

On the basis of these two ideas, Maritain wrote his massive *L'humanisme intégrale* in 1936, which carried on an open dialogue with modernity. Recognizing the new context for Catholic social teaching and relying on his understanding of the human person, he offered Catholic arguments in support of political democracy and religious and ideological pluralism. He argued that the dignity of human beings demands that society recognizes their freedom to define themselves and allows them to be co-responsible for the common good. Maritain's arguments, we note, were not drawn from the liberal tradition, based on utilitarian reason; instead, he grounded democracy on the transcendent vocation of human beings, an insight based on metaphysical reason. It deserves to be remembered that traditional societies did not recognize the transcendent dignity of the human person: they saw persons as embedded in a hierarchical community where their honour was recognized according to different levels of dignity.

In 1943, while a refugee in New York City, Maritain published *Christianisme et démocratie*,[25] in which he defended the liberal ideas of democratic pluralism and human rights as secularized values derived from the teaching of Jesus.

We noted that Maritain used two intellectual strategies to rethink and change the Church's official social doctrine. First, he turned to the universal dimension of the Church's teaching, its metaphysical understanding of human persons living in community; second, he recognized the contextual character of the Church's social doctrine and argued that in the present context, the traditional teaching must be rethought and reformulated. These two intellectual strategies – the turn to the universal and the attention to context – are also used, as we shall see, in the Muslim theology of Tariq Ramadan.

Pope John XXIII and after

Pope John XXIII added a new argument – beyond Maritain's philosophy – in support of democracy and human rights. The pope had been deeply affected by the horrors committed during World War II, and admired the subsequent Universal Declaration of Human Rights promulgated by the United Nations in 1948. He regarded these events as "signs of the times" – events that may not be overlooked or taken for granted but that demand to be interpreted in the light of the Gospel. Like many thinking Catholics at the time, John XXIII was deeply troubled by the Church's official teaching, which still repudiated human rights and the principle of religious liberty. Error had no rights, according to the traditional teaching. John XXIII decided to return to the Scriptures and hear anew God's Word addressed to the Church. He tells us in his encyclical *Pacem in terris* (1943) that he found revealed in the Bible the high dignity of each human being, the foundation of their human rights and their religious liberty. First, according to the book of Genesis, humans were created in the image of God.[26] Second, according to the Pauline letters, all human beings are called to be friends of God through Christ's death and resurrection.[27] Implicit in the biblical teaching of creation and redemption is the transcendent dignity of the human person that society must respect and protect by an appropriate legislation.

This biblical argument confirms the rational philosophical reflection offered by John XXIII:

> Any human society, if it is to be well-ordered and productive, must lay down as a foundation the principle that all human beings are persons, endowed by nature with intelligence and free will, and that, for this reason, they have rights and duties that flow directly from their nature. These rights are universal, inviolable and inalienable.[28]

We note that in addition to the two intellectual strategies, the turn to the universal and the attention to context, John XXIII added a third one: the return to Scripture. We shall see that Tariq Ramadan also uses these three intellectual moves.

After a long, painful and passionate debate, the Second Vatican Council endorsed the papal teaching in the conciliar Declaration of Religious Liberty.[29] The opposition of many bishops from traditional Catholic countries and many members of the Roman Curia made an enormous effort to prevent the Council from defending the freedom of religion. Since I worked as a theologian at the Unity

Secretariat under Cardinal Bea, the body that produced the draft proposals on ecumenism, religious pluralism and the freedom of religion, I remember the vehement opposition to religious liberty on the part of a significant sector of the Council. These bishops argued that the Catholic Church could not propose a teaching that had been repeatedly condemned by the popes in the nineteenth and early 20th century. Our reply to them was that the world we now lived in had changed, and it demanded the rethinking of previous teaching. Without the passionate involvement of the American bishops, the draft proposal for the Declaration on Religious Liberty might never have been submitted to the Council. The public debate on the council floor eventually convinced the great majority of bishops and ultimately produced an almost unanimous support for the Declaration. Pope Paul VI, who had succeeded John XXIII, was still nervous. He sent the official text to his old acquaintance Jacques Maritain, asking for his advice.[30] After receiving Maritain's approval, Paul VI promulgated the Declaration on December 7, 1965.

In the 1980s and '90s, Pope John Paul II became increasingly disturbed by the economic, cultural and military conflicts that destabilized global society and produced massacres in several parts of the world. After the collapse of the Soviet Union and end of the Cold War, new conflicts emerged that produced violent outbursts, regional wars and military aggression. Reflecting on these signs of the times in the light of the Gospel, John Paul II interpreted the Church's mission primarily as promoting peace and justice in the world, in cooperation with the world religions and secular ethical traditions. He produced a remarkable document called "Ten Commandments for Peace," which reconciles the Church to the religious and cultural pluralism of the world and summons all peoples to seek global peace through dialogue and cooperation.[31]

Economic liberalism

Up to this point, we have considered the Church's reaction to political liberalism. I now wish to make a few remarks about the Church's reaction to economic liberalism, because the Catholic teaching on economic justice, its critique of liberal and neo-liberal capitalism, and its solidarity with the poor nations of the South are similar to, if not identical to, the Islamic social ethics proposed by Tariq Ramadan.

It is well known that for over 1,500 years, the Church regarded as gravely sinful the receipt of payment for loaning money. Usury, as it was called, was also forbidden in Islam. John Calvin was the first Christian theologian who argued that because the role of money in society had changed, it was ethically admissible to take interest on capital loaned to entrepreneurs. Eventually, the Catholic Church reconciled itself to the emerging capitalism, yet it continued to denounce economic activities unrestrained by ethical norms.

Beginning with Leo XIII's encyclical *Rerum novarum* (1891), the Church's belated response to industrial capitalism, the popes developed what came to be called the Church's social doctrine. This important body of literature

offers an ongoing analysis of the social and economic injustices in capitalist and communist societies, and proposes
ethical principles, the application of which would make
society more just, more humane and more participatory.
I have dealt with the Church's social teaching in several
publications.[32] Over the years, especially under John Paul
II, the Church's critique of liberal and neo-liberal capitalism
has become very bold. While markets are invaluable human
inventions, they must be regulated to serve the common
good of society. To surrender the well-being of society
simply to the laws of the market is wholly irrational. Many
needs cannot be delivered by the market; many goods may
not be bought and sold. According to John Paul II, markets
must be constrained to serve the whole of society by a set
of laws, a strong labour movement and a culture of solidarity, a spiritual task.

Since Tariq Ramadan's *tiers-mondisme* has been criticized
in France as opportunistic and unrelated to his interpretation of Islam,[33] I wish to recall that the conversion to the
third-world perspective on the part of the Catholic Church
occurred with Pope Paul VI's 1967 encyclical, *Populorum
progressio*. The economic inequality between the North and
the South, writes Paul VI, is a situation whose "injustice
cries to heaven."[34] Countries of the North cannot achieve
a truthful knowledge of themselves unless they take into
account their exploitative relationship with the South.

These brief remarks on economic liberalism reveal
that the Church's reconciliation with political liberalism
(democracy, pluralism and human rights) does not imply

that the Church is naively uncritical of modern society. On the contrary, the Church sees in liberal capitalism an economic system that concedes uncontrolled power to the rich, produces an ethos of individualism and utilitarianism, and generates an eager desire for material goods, leading to spiritual emptiness. From the Catholic point of view, liberalism defined by the maxim *liberté, égalité, fraternité* has betrayed fraternity by undermining the traditions and institutions that promote solidarity. For this reason, the Church's openness to modernity is a highly critical openness – supporting democracy, pluralism and human rights while denouncing the institutional and cultural forces that sin against justice and solidarity. We shall see in subsequent chapters that Tariq Ramadan's openness to political modernity is also a highly critical openness.

2

TARIQ RAMADAN'S LOCATION
ON THE ISLAMIC SPECTRUM

The contemporary reader is keenly aware that Christianity represents a wide spectrum of religious thought and practice. Not only is there a range of churches and confessions, but within each of these are found various trends of theology and piety. We take for granted that to understand a Christian theologian we must place him or her in the Christian tradition in which he or she is situated. The contemporary reader is also aware that Judaism exists in a variety of "confessions": Orthodox, Conservative, Reformed, Hasidic and Reconstructionist. What is much less understood is the complex theological spectrum of Islam. Newspapers have invented the distinction between moderate and extremist Muslims, which is unsatisfactory, unrelated as it is to the complex history of Islam.

Tariq Ramadan recognizes that to understand his theology it is necessary to have a certain knowledge of the history of Islam and know where he himself locates his thought within this historical development. He tells this to his non-Muslim readers, most of whom have little knowledge of Islam. He tells this more emphatically to his Muslim readers, whom he wants to convince that his theology is in keeping with the Islamic tradition. Since Muslims may feel that his ideas are unduly influenced by modernity and thus deviate from the inherited religion, Ramadan insists that a certain knowledge of Islamic history is necessary if a Muslim wants to discover what fidelity to Islam means in modern society. For this reason, Ramadan begins his book *To Be a European Muslim* with a chapter on the development of Islamic thought and practice, showing both the bold creativity and, at other times, the passive conformity of this religious tradition. A survey of this development is necessary if we want to understand where in this story Ramadan locates himself.

A historical overview

609–632: Revelation to the Prophet
632–61: The Rightly Guided Caliphs
661–750: The Umayyad Dynasty
750–1258: The Abbasid Dynasty (750–850: The Great Imams)

The starting point of Islam is the divine revelation to the Prophet Muhammad (570–632) over a period of 23 years. This revelation of the one true God was a new and provocative message among the Arabian tribes that practised a polytheistic religion and engaged in perpetuated tribal hostilities. Muhammad succeeded in uniting the Arabs in the faith of the one and only God (*tahwid*). Yet, from another point of view, the Quranic revelation was not new at all: it recalled and confirmed the revelation that God had granted to prophets in the past, especially those of the biblical tradition, including Abraham, Moses and Jesus. More than that, according to the Quran, the revelation of God as Creator and Sustainer of the universe confirms the rational intuition of human beings as they reflect on their experience of the world. So that God's self-revelation be continually remembered and become the authoritative guide of people's lives, the Prophet was instructed to introduce a set of rites to be practised by Muslims. These rites are the five pillars of Islam:

i)　the public witness to the one God,
ii)　the ritual prayer five times a day,
iii)　the alms given to the poor,
iv)　the fast during the month of Ramadan, and
v)　the pilgrimage to Mecca once during one's lifetime.

The Quran also reveals principles of the good life that will make the community of believers (*umma*) peace-loving and just.

With other contemporary Muslim religious thinkers,[35] Ramadan insists that the Islam revealed in the Quran was essentially a religious ethos, a call to the worship of God and a guide to a holy way of life in community. Only a small number of verses legislate human behaviour. Ramadan's *In the Footsteps of the Prophet*[36] shows the wisdom and spirituality of Muhammad and the common sense he relied upon in the guidance of his community. The perception of the Quran as the divine revelation of a way of life affects Ramadan's entire theological project.

With Muhammad's death in 632, a period of foundational importance for the interpretation of the Quranic revelation began. Between 632 and 661, the leadership of the believing community was successively exercised by four caliphs, or vicars – Abu Bakr, Umar, Utman, and Ali – elected from among the Prophet's close friends and associates, called his Companions. The caliphs wanted to be faithful to God's revelation; they followed the example of Muhammad and relied on this revelation as they guided the lives of the faithful and governed their community. They also saw to it that the oral recitation of the Quran was transcribed in a single book as the definitive sacred text for the entire Muslim community. In subsequent years, Muslims referred to these leaders as the four "rightly guided caliphs."

Under their leadership, Islam reveals its spiritual creativity. Tariq Ramadan shows that in those years, fidelity to the Quran did not create a culture of conformity. Already the Prophet had recognized that if practical matters were not settled by the revelation he had received, the responsible leaders were to use their common sense. When the Prophet sent Muadh ibn Jabal, a leader in the community, as an emissary to settle a conflict in Yemen, the Prophet gave him the following advice: when divine revelation does not provide a clear rule of what is to be done in a particular situation, he should use his own careful judgment.[37] A new historical context demanded an appropriate response, an intelligent application of the Quranic wisdom. Ramadan reminds his readers that, during a severe famine, Caliph Umar, recognizing that people were stealing food to survive, made the decision that the severe punishment reserved for thieves was not to be applied.[38] The creative interpretation of the Quran by the Prophet's Companions – as we shall see further on – inspired the Islamic reform movement, al-nahda, beginning at the end of the nineteenth century. Ramadan locates himself in this theological movement.

Yet the 29 years under the rightly guided caliphs was not free of conflicts within the community. At the end of this period, a dramatic quarrel took place. Muslims remember it as the great fitna. After the death of Caliph Ali, Muawiya of the Umayyad tribe, then the governor of Syria, refused to acknowledge Ali's son, Husayn, as the new legitimate caliph. The conflict culminated in a battle in which Husayn was killed. As the new caliph, Muawiya imposed a strict regime on the community, inspired less by fidelity to the Quran than by the consolidation of his power. The partisans of Ali and Husayn decided to break away from the community. Their followers regarded Ali as the only genuine caliph, mourned the violent death of Husayn, and entertained the hope of divine guidance offered by a holy successor. What took place at the end of the formative period of Islam (632–661) was the tragic schism between the majority, the Sunni, who recognized the four rightly guided caliphs, and the minority, the Shia, who refused to concede them recognition. Both the Sunni and the Shia accept the Quran as God's definitive self-revelation: despite their different views

of the caliphs, they practise the same religion and profess
the unity of Islam.

With Muawiya began the Umayyad Era of Islam (661–
750). Muslim historians tend to look upon this period in a
critical manner. Ramadan shares their evaluation. He recalls
that Muawiya, relying on Byzantine, Persian and Indian
models, transformed the caliphate into a hereditary king-
ship. What was abandoned here, Ramadan writes, was the
practice of consultation or *shura* that had been a constant
feature of the governance exercised by the Prophet and the
rightly guided caliphs. Muawiya also converted the com-
munal treasury into the personal property of the caliph and
his family.[39] The Umayyad caliphs lived the luxurious lives
of royalty, largely indifferent to the Islamic ethos.

Muawiya regarded as his principal aim the creation of
a legal system based on Islamic principles that would unite
and stabilize his growing realm. He assigned this task to a
team of jurists who sought to derive these laws from passages in the Quran and the practice of the Prophet. These
religious jurists, the *ulama*, became the authentic guardians
of the Quran. It was not the caliph, but they, the *ulama*,
who exercised religious authority in the community. Here
politics and religion moved apart.

Since the task assigned to the *ulama* was the making of
law, they interpreted the Quran largely in legal terms, speci-
fying what actions were allowed, recommended, tolerated
or strictly forbidden. The *ulama* were not theologians who
explored the meaning of the Quranic passages; they were

jurists who made explicit the rules and laws (*fiqh*) implicit in the Quran.

Another development during the Umayyad Era was the collection of the *hadith*, the words or actions of the Prophet as remembered by his close associates. The *ulama* who collected these memories also investigated whether they were reported by reliable witnesses and whether the memories agreed with the teaching of the Quran. They found it necessary to distinguish between the authentic and inauthentic *hadith*, and even assigned varying degrees of authority to the authentic ones. Thanks to the work of these scholars, the divine revelation in which Muslims believe is handed on in their history through the Quran and the authentic traditions, called the Sunna.

What emerges in the Umayyad Era is the developments of systematic fields of research, referred to as "the Islamic sciences," that include legal interpretation (*fiqh*), the collecting and sifting of *hadith*, and several other inquiries into the normative guidance provided by the Quran to Muslim life in community. In *To Be a European Muslim*, Ramadan describes the Islamic sciences in some detail.[40] What does not become perfectly clear, as we shall see, is how he relates his own theology to these sciences.

Muslim historians regard the shift to a new dynasty, the Abbasid caliphate, in 750 as an important event with profound religious significance. During the first hundred years, the caliphs of this dynasty were intelligent religious leaders. Known as the "great imams," they were well versed in the Islamic tradition and created the conditions for the cultural

flourishing of the Muslim community. Ramadan mentions
the further development of the Islamic sciences, the free
discussion of theological ideas, the emergence of several
centres of thought, and the dialogue of Muslim thinkers
with the Greek and Persian intellectual traditions.

Ramadan refers especially to the development of different schools of juridical interpretation, a process already
begun in the Umayyad Era. This development became
necessary because of the ongoing expansion of the Islamic
realm, which was made up of diverse cultures, and the need
to interpret the Quran in response to distinct regional situations. Among these schools of law, four assumed special
importance: the Hanafi, Malaki, Shafii and Hanbali. The
Hanafi tradition is the most liberal, allowing more than the
others a contextual interpretation of the Quran.

In the cosmopolitan atmosphere during the early years
of the Abbasid Era, Muslim intellectuals in dialogue with
classical Greek philosophies became convinced of the harmony existing between human reason and divine revelation.
Muhammad had insisted that God's revealed Word was
confirmed by thoughtful reflection on the experience of the
world. He had spoken of the world as "the second book"
revealing the one true God. Now, encouraged by Hellenistic
philosophy, a group of theologians – the Mutazila – argued
not only that divine revelation was confirmed by reason, but
that reason itself led to the knowledge of God's existence
and the recognition of God's unique power and wisdom.
This development marked the entry of philosophy into the
Muslim tradition.[41] By a historical coincidence, Caliph al-

Mamun and his successors (815–847) adopted the teaching of the Mutazila as the official orthodoxy and persecuted the conservative thinkers, a policy that provoked the opposition of the people deeply attached to the inherited piety. Some of the Mutazila may well have exaggerated the independent competence of reason and promoted a rationalism at odds with the transcendent nature of God's wisdom revealed in the Quran. A new caliph then changed the public policy: the Mutazila theology was condemned and the traditional piety, suspicious of reason, became the official position.

Despite the condemnation, the Mutazila inheritance continued to haunt the Islamic tradition. A century after these events, Abu al-Ashari (d. 935) offered a reconciliation between the philosophical approach of the Mutazila and the traditionalism hostile to philosophy. Al-Ashari recognized that divine revelation was confirmed by reason and in harmony with the intelligent reflection on human experience, but he denied that human intelligence offered an independent way of encountering the God of revelation.

A certain suspicion of philosophy remained alive in the Muslim tradition. In subsequent centuries, the well-known philosophers Al-Farabi (d. 950), Ibn Sina [Avicenna] (d. 1037) and Ibn Rochd [Averroes] (d. 1198) were condemned as heretical by the powerful juridical schools.

The Abbasid Era also saw the emergence of the Sufi tradition, the ascetical and mystical way inspired by the Quran. One of the founders of this current was a woman, Rabia al-Adawwiya (d. 766). Some of the Sufis, organized as religious orders, went so far as to claim that their close union with God dispensed them from following the rules and rituals of Islam. This claim was repudiated by the spokesmen for the juridical schools. Even the idea of union with God was looked upon with a certain suspicion by the defenders of orthodoxy: believers were called to surrender themselves to God's will, yet the God whom they obeyed remained forever unreachable. The Muslim scholar Abu Hamid Al-Gazzali (d. 1111), a Sufi himself, is regarded by many Muslim historians as the great religious thinker who was able to protect the unity of Islam by reconciling the Sufi tradition with the legal Islam as defined by the great schools, and by repudiating the independent intellectual inquiry of the philosophers. Al-Gazzali presented Islam as the middle way, tolerant of the various trends within the believing community, respectful of the cultural pluralism created by the vast extent of the Muslim world, obedient to the revealed law as interpreted by the major schools of law, and open to the ascetical/mystical tradition founded upon the Quran.[42]

In the meantime, the Muslim world was losing its political unity. By 960, certain regions, such as Egypt and Andalusia, had made themselves more or less independent. The Abbasid caliphate was no longer universally recognized, and consequently lost the authority to settle the questions raised by religious disagreements. The Abbasid dynasty continued to rule in the Middle East until 1248, the year of the destructive invasion of the Mongols. Yet from 950 on, binding religious authority was again exercised by the *ulama*, the jurists of great schools of law and the thinkers steeped in the Sufi tradition. A clear separation was taking place between the political and the religious orders. Religion still demanded obedience to the legitimate rulers, but the ruler no longer defended the right interpretation of the Quran. Because of the expanding cultural pluralism and the absence of a single voice of authority, the *ulama*, fearful that error might contaminate the Quranic truth, became increasingly conservative. They rejected fresh Quranic interpretations (*ijtihad*) that responded to new historical events or tried to resolve debates in the believing community. They claimed that "the doors of ijtihad" were now closed. The dominant conservatism made Islam for many centuries into a religion of conformity, unable to respond to the challenges of history. This changed only at the end of the nineteenth century with the start of the renewal movement (*al-nadah*).

Ramadan evaluates the history of the juridical interpretation of the Quran, beginning in 750, in this way:

Flowering	Consolidation	Stagnation and Decline	The Renewal
750–960	960–1258	1258–1870	1870– [43]

The renewal movement

Six hundred years of stagnation and decline: this is a harsh judgment on the history of Islam. Ramadan is by no means the only Muslim intellectual who offers this negative evaluation. This judgment is part of the wake-up call of the renewal movement, *al-nadah*, started by Jamal al-Afghani (d. 1897) in the second half of the nineteenth century. This renewal movement, also called the reform, summoned

Muslims to wrestle against the colonial domination imposed by the Western powers, yet the reform did not put the blame for the lack of cultural creativity of the Muslim world on Western colonialism. The movement criticized the individualism, materialism and secularism produced by Western modernity, yet its main emphasis was on the need for Muslim self-criticism. The principal reason for the decline of the Muslim societies, al-Afghani argued, was the stagnation of Islam, its conservative spirit, its indifference to social inequality, and its suspicion of modern science.

The complaints of al-Afghani were many. He lamented that cultural practices and popular superstitions had obscured the original message of Islam. He argued that Muslims had become imprisoned in a purely legalistic interpretation of Islam, slaves of conservative jurists indifferent to contemporary experience. He also criticized the Muslim rulers for their indifference to their people's well-being and for neglecting to foster their education. While critical of Western empire, al-Afghani urged Muslims to study Western science and become innovative scientists themselves. Despite his struggle against colonial domination, he never adopted an anti-Western ideology. He wanted Muslims to learn from what he considered the great achievements of the West. He argued that, in its original purity, the Islam proclaimed and practised by the Prophet and his Companions was open to human reason and capable of creative responses to new historical challenges. While many Muslims questioned the orthodoxy of al-Afghani, he himself believed that returning to the teaching of the Quran was a theological approach fully respected by the Islamic sciences.

Al-Afghani travelled all over the Muslim world: he gave public lectures in the great cities, produced articles addressed to educated believers, founded reviews that encouraged Muslim intellectuals to express themselves in public, and involved himself in diplomatic efforts to influence the policies of Muslim rulers. He started a renewal movement in Islam that was taken up and developed by his disciples, beginning with his friend, the Egyptian scholar Muhammad Abdou (d. 1905). A careful study of this movement under the title *Aux sources du renouveau musulman*[44] was published by Tariq Ramadan. In it he introduces the reader to the thought and practice of Jamal al-Afghani, Muhammad Abdou and a series of religious leaders from various parts of the Muslim world.

I wish to make three remarks about this important book. Ramadan shows that with Muhammad Abdou, the renewal moves in a slightly different direction. Writing at a time when there was still some hope for the recovery of the Ottoman Empire, al-Afghani had addressed himself to the intellectual and political elite, and even sought to exercise direct influence upon the governing authorities. By contrast, Mohammad Abdou and the subsequent reformers believed that the renewal had to start with the people, the believing men and women. These reformers stressed the education of the people: they wanted them to discover for themselves the religious meaning of Islam, be transformed by their faith and become actors in society, seeking to make

it conform to the Islamic ideal of justice and peace. The
renewal movement now tried to transform society from
below: it urged the believers to create centres, networks,
publications and institutions to influence public opinion.
The reformist thinkers hoped that renewed faith in Islam
would affect what social scientists call civil society; they
did not envisage an Islamic state, they opposed the idea of
imposing faith and virtue from above, they believed that
the time of personal freedom had arrived. They also recognized the socio-political dimension of Islam, the creation
of a just and peace-loving society, also a transformation to
be brought about from below.

The second remark has to do with Ramadan's interpretation of Hassan al-Banna, the founder of the Muslim Brotherhood. Ramadan presents him as an important thinker and
actor of the renewal movement: rereading the Quran and
the Sunna, linking faith and social justice, advocating the
free discussion of ideas, attempting to transform Egyptian
society from below, and advocating non-violent action
– with one exception: supporting the military defence
of Palestine. In a long section – 211 pages, to be precise
– Ramadan analyzes al-Banna's writings, most of which
have not been translated into English or French. Since
the Muslim Brotherhood presented a serious challenge to
the Egyptian government and the established elites, they
eventually suffered repression, and Hassan al-Banna himself was murdered in 1949. It was only afterwards, in the
prisons of President Nasser, that the Muslim Brotherhood
became deeply divided, some – supported by Sayyed

Qutb – recommended the use of violence; others remained faithful to the al-Banna's original vision.

Not all readers have been convinced by Ramadan's analysis. Some historians of Islam regard the Muslim Brotherhood as an organization that, from the beginning, was opposed not only to the ruling elites, but also to the Western ideals of pluralism and democracy. For some, the Muslim Brotherhood is a dangerously violent organization; for other observers, it is an unjustly oppressed social movement. The ample literature on the Muslim Brotherhood has not arrived at an unanimous evaluation.[45] Ramadan offers a positive interpretation of Hassan al-Banna (who was his grandfather): he sees him as a thinker and actor belonging to the renewal movement, committed to popular education and resistance to colonialism. In conversation with scholars who disagree with him, Ramadan offers a set of arguments drawn from al-Banna's writings. The hostile propaganda against Ramadan in France has used his intellectual solidarity with al-Banna to suggest that Ramadan is associated with the Muslim Brotherhood and shares their supposed political aim: the creation of a Muslim state. While Ramadan's brother has a certain connection with the Muslim Brotherhood, Tariq Ramadan has no association whatever with that organization. Nor does he think – as we shall see in detail – that the Quran calls for the creation of an Islamic state. If his interpretation of al-Banna's writings is overly benevolent, this calls for a scholarly debate, not for accusations of subversion.

A third remark has to do with a topic of Islamic fun-
damentalism, briefly discussed in *Aux sources du renouveau
musulman*. The renewal movement initiated by al-Afghani
was not the only reaction to the decline of Muslim societies
and the stagnation of Islam: there also occurred a reaction of
conservative religious leaders who denounced the absence
of fervour among the faithful, their indifference to the divine summons and their lax interpretation of Islamic law.
The dominant Islamic culture, they argued, resembled the
religious confusion that the Prophet encountered among
the Arabs of his day and that God corrected and overcame
through the revelation of the Quran. In the eighteenth
century, Muhammad ibn-Abd al-Wahhab (d. 1792), preaching in Arabia, had warned against the spread of idolatry,
denounced as corrupt the Islam practised in the cultural
centres of the Muslim world, and called for the conversion
of Muslims to the faith and practice of the Prophet and his
Companions. His literalist reading of the Quran convinced
him that Muslims had to return to the Islamic way of life
of the seventh century. Wahhab's interpretation of Islam
won the respect of the Saudi family, which, in the early
nineteenth century, founded the Kingdom of Saudi Arabia.
The Saudi family remained faithful to Wahhabism and
used its ample oil revenues to spread fundamentalist Islam
throughout the whole of the Muslim world. This sectarian, puritan Islam is hostile to art, to the intellectual life, to
dialogue with other theological trends, and in particularly
to Western civilization. Yet Wahhabism is normally committed to a non-violent struggle.

Related to Wahhabism, yet much more problematic, are certain radical Muslim thinkers and leaders who, from the second part of the 20th century on, offer a literalist, non-contextual reading of the Quranic passages that call for violent action to defend the truth. Ramadan denounces the use of religion to legitimate violence. In his writings he does not disguise the fundamentalist face of Islam, nor does he remain silent in the face of religious-based terrorism. He analyzes the thought of the radical religious leaders and names the organizations that they have started. [46]

A classification of current trends

Ramadan sees himself as belonging to the renewal movement initiated by al-Afghani. What is special about Ramadan is that he addresses Muslims living in the West, while the early reformist thinkers addressed Muslims living in traditionally Islamic societies. Ramadan is aware that Western Muslims are constantly exposed by the mass media to images of exotic Islam and rigid Muslim personalities who despise Western civilization. It is therefore important for Western Muslims, he argues, to have a clear idea of the various tendencies in contemporary Islam. The distinction made in the Western media between radical and moderate Muslims offers little insight in the complexity of contemporary Islam. Ramadan presents a more accurate classification of the various currents in today's worldwide Muslim community, and he shows where he and the renewal movement fit into the wider picture.[47] To understand this classification, it is necessary to have a certain acquaintance with the history of Islamic thought and practice. That is why the first and longer part of the present chapter has offered an overview of this historical development.

1. Ramadan calls the first tendency *scholastic traditionalism*. Muslims who belong to this current practise Islam in strict conformity with the jurisdictional decisions (*fiqh*) made by one of the major schools of law founded during the ninth and tenth centuries. These Muslims accept the decision of the *ulama* of the tenth century that "the doors of *ijtihad* "have been closed," and for this reason do not search the Quran and the Sunna for fresh insights. Because of their inflexible understanding of Islam, they regard Western modernity as a major threat to their faith. Many of them become rigid in their traditionalism. To symbolize their resistance to the West, they emphasize obedience to the external forms of worship, the dress code and various religious practices laid down in the past by the jurists of a particular jurisdictional school. According to Ramadan, in the West, rigid traditionalism is particularly strong in England among Indo-Pakistani Muslims and in Germany among the Turks. These Muslims resist integration into the society in which they live: they try instead to create their own Islamic subculture. In the East, this tendency sometimes produces extremely narrow expressions of Islam. According to Ramadan, the Taliban of Afghanistan belong to this current.

2. *Salafi traditionalism* is the second current – I prefer to call it *literalism* – which is often confused with the above-mentioned legalistic trend. What characterizes Salafi traditionalism is the desire to practise the Islam announced

and lived by the Prophet Muhammad and his "Salafi," or Companions. Muslims in this current go directly to the Quran and the Sunna without the mediation of the traditional schools of law. They read the sacred texts in a naively literal manner without taking into account their historical context or the author's intention. This literalism, as we saw above, began to flourish as a reaction to the passivity and lack of fervour exhibited by scholastic traditionalism. Wahhabism belongs to this current. Muslims in this current regard the legal judgments made by the Islamic sciences as compromises and falsifications. Interpretation, they believe, leads to innovation and heresy (*bida*). Needless to say, the literalists do not search in the Quran for new insights that could shed light on the present historical situation.

3. Ramadan calls the third tendency *Salafi reformism*. This refers to the Islamic renewal movement (*al-nahda*), initiated by al-Afghani and carried forward by Muslim thinkers and leaders in many parts. This is the current in which Ramadan locates his own theory and practice. Muslims in this current refuse to be locked into the judgments and interpretations made by the Islamic schools of law between the eighth and tenth centuries. They prefer to return to the Islam practised by the Prophet and his "Salafi," or Companions – an Islam that was open to reason and common sense and capable of responding creatively to historical challenges. These Muslims hold that "the doors of *ijtihad*" are open: rereading the Quran and the Sunna by taking into account the historical context and the author's intention, they search in the sacred sources insights that will illumine their contemporary expe-

rience. They argue that *ijtihad* is in fact a perpetual practice that allows Muslims to remain faithful to God's Word in a new historical context.

What is the relation of the Islamic renewal movement (*Salafi reformism*) to the Islamic schools of law? Here Ramadan is not perfectly clear. On the one hand, he asserts that in reading the Quran, reformist thinkers are not prisoners of the *fiqh* offered by the jurisdictional schools: these thinkers go directly to the sacred sources, use reason to interpret the sacred texts, and thus listen to God's Word in full awareness of their own historical situation. On the other hand, if I am not mistaken, Ramadan interprets the sacred sources in accordance with hermeneutical principles that are recognized in the Islamic sciences. This means that he does not want to think theologically in total independence of the classical juridical schools. The subsequent chapters will show that Ramadan's theology is innovative and even bold, and at the same time respectful of tradition, using the legal discourse to which Muslims are accustomed.

According to Ramadan, the renewal movement is having a profound influence upon Muslim communities in the countries of East and West. Muslims are grateful to find in the movement an emphasis on rationality, on personal freedom and on doing God's will in the world. Because theologians of *al-nahda* want to remain faithful to the Quran and insist that their rereading of the Quran, while new, is sanctioned by tradition, they are sometimes accused by secular commentators of being fundamentalists in disguise. This has happened to Ramadan many times. In my study of the Turkish religious thinkers Said Nursi and Fethullah Gülen, brilliant representatives of the Islamic renewal, I have discovered that this also happened to them.[48] Even though they defended democratic pluralism in theological terms, they were suspected by secular politicians of being Islamists in disguise, plotting to create an Islamic state.

4. The small but well-publicized fourth current of recent origin is what Ramadan refers to as *political Salafiyya*, and I prefer to call *politicized literalism*. This current has been created by Muslims located in literalism or in the renewal, who had experienced repression and imprisonment by dictatorial Muslim rulers. In anger and despair, they decided to practise a purely political reading of the Quran, rejected as corrupt the religion of Muslim rulers and their societies, and defined Western civilization as an inveterate enemy of Islam. They bracketed the Quran's ethical teaching on humility, justice and peace, and instead focused on passages that record the Prophet's defensive military action against the hostile Arabian tribes that threatened the existence of his small community. The politicized literalists yearn for the creation of the Islamic state, promote hostility to Western empire and plot against Muslim governments that have friendly relations with the West. In *To Be a European Muslim*, published in 2005, Ramadan writes that this current represents "less than 0.5 % of the Muslim population resident in Europe."[49]

5. The fifth tendency is *liberal reformism*, which is also referred to as *modernism*. This current is supported by Muslims who embrace the ideas and values of the Western

Enlightenment. They are convinced that to make Islam relevant to modern society, it is necessary to submit the Islamic tradition to the critique of contemporary rationality. They hold that God's revelation in the Quran presents above all a religious ethos, a summons to divine worship and the virtuous life of individuals and communities. The legal interpretation offered by the Islamic schools of law, they think, has lost its relevance. While they believe that God's Word is made known in the Quran, they look upon the Quran also as human book, the writing and editing of which should be studied scientifically. Modernity, they think, calls for a certain break with tradition. This current is widely spread and supported by important intellectuals in the old Muslim world and, more especially, in the countries of the West. Many Muslims drift into this tendency and – so Ramadan fears – gradually become purely secular in outlook. Ramadan defends human rights and democratic pluralism in the name of his Quranic faith, but he does not see himself as a modernist. For him, the difference between the renewal movement and liberal Islam is significant. (In chapter 6 of this book, we shall take a closer look at his argument with liberal Muslim scholars.)

6. The sixth tendency mentioned by Ramadan is *Sufism*, practised in a variety of forms throughout traditional Muslim countries and the rest of the world. Sufi Muslims concentrate on the Quranic passages that stress ascetical practices, God's nearness to the soul, and the need to surrender to God in one's heart. Sufism represents the mystical dimension of Islam. In the past, Sufis often belonged to

separate orders or brotherhoods, and sometimes rejected the legal dimension of Islam altogether. Today, Sufis follow their mystical vocation while observing the rules and external obligations of Islam. There is spiritual Sufi influence among many Muslims who do not regard themselves as Sufis: they want to cultivate the spiritual life, recognizing that it helps them to do what Islam demands of them, namely to struggle against their selfishness. In my study of Turkish Islam, I learned that Sufism has been an important current in Anatolia, and that the whole of Turkish Islam has been marked by the Sufi tradition.

Ramadan's analysis of contemporary Islam and the declaration of where his own thought is located on this spectrum offer indispensable help for understanding his theology.

3

THE UNIVERSAL MESSAGE OF ISLAM

The arrival of modernity has been a challenge for all religious traditions. In chapter 1, we saw that the Catholic tradition wrestled for over a century before it supported democratic pluralism and human rights. In chapter 2, we encountered the renewal movement in Islam that found in the Quran resources for respecting the political institutions of modernity. Tariq Ramadan belongs to this movement. He addresses himself specifically to Muslims living in the West. It is imperative for them to know how to relate themselves on the basis of their faith to the structures of pluralism and democracy. The first important step Ramadan takes is to introduce a distinction between the particular and the universal message of Islam.

The divine revelation granted to the Prophet Muhammad summoned the population of the Arab Peninsula, which was deeply divided into hostile tribes, to trust and worship the one God and to constitute a just and peaceful society pleasing to Him. The tribes had been in perpetual violent conflict, driven in part by their polytheistic religious beliefs: competition among the gods here produced hostility among the worshipers. In this historical situation, the Quranic revelation of the one true God produced a religious, cultural and political revolution. The one true God who has no companion, *tahwid*, is the principal proclamation of Islam: it is the profound source from which flow the revealed directives for the holy life in community. Muhammad was appointed to introduce the worship of the One God in Arabia, wrestle against polytheistic beliefs and rituals, and reconcile the Arab population in a just and law-abiding community. The Prophet and his followers saw themselves as Muslims – as persons obedient to God. They surrendered themselves to the divine will, worshipping God and creating a holy community (*umma*) as instructed.

In addition to the particular message addressed to Muslims, the Quran also contains a universal message revealing the origin, meaning and destiny of human life and the cosmos. The Quranic revelation of *tahwid* addresses human reason, assuming that men and women reflecting on their experience of the world will confirm the existence of the one true God. Disclosed in the Quran is a religious interpretation of human and cosmic existence that human intelligence, touched by God, is able to understand. "Prophet, do you not see that all those who are in the heavens and earth praise God, as do the birds with wings outstretched? ... Control of the heavens and earth belongs to God and to God is the final return. Do you not see that God drives the clouds, then gathers them together and piles them up until you see rain from their midst? ... God has power over

everything" (Quran 24:41-43, 45). It is this revealed world
view that Ramadan presents as the stepping stone for his
theology.[50]

Faith and reason

The universal meaning of the Quran may not have pre-
occupied the first generations of Muslims. But when, a century after the death of the Prophet, Muslims living in Syria
and Iraq encountered the Greek and Persian intellectual
traditions, they realized that the Quran summoned human
beings to use their intelligence, reflect on their experience
of the world, and articulate the world view implicit in God's
revealed Word. Muslims came to recognize the affinity
between divine revelation and human intelligence. The
Mutazila school may have gone too far in suggesting that
unaided human reason could reach the truths revealed in the
Quran. But, as we saw in chapter 2, the theological debate
was eventually settled by the widely accepted teaching of
Abu al-Ashari. According to this teaching, divine revelation is confirmed by human reason and thus has a certain
affinity with human intelligence, even if human reason,
being finite and fallible, stands in need of enlightenment
by divine revelation.

The word *theology* is not used a great deal by Muslim
thinkers, even though some of them refer to it as *kalam*.
Ramadan argues that Christians developed theologies and
engaged in theological controversies because they had to
make sense of the opaque biblical teaching regarding God
Father, Son and Holy Spirit.[51] The Quranic revelation of the

Oneness of God, *tawhid*, Ramadan argues, is more rational: it speaks to human reason and hence did not provoke long controversies in the Muslim community.

Ramadan mentions another reason why *kalam* was not a mayor preoccupation of Muslim intellectuals. The *ulama* and the Islamic schools of law preferred to concentrate on the juridical implications of the Quran, rather than explore and develop the ideas revealed in the sacred text. Many contemporary Muslim thinkers wish to correct this. Tariq Ramadan's own articulation of the Quran's universal message constitutes a theology of human and cosmic existence based on God's revealed Word.

Universal revelation

We mentioned earlier that the Prophet Muhammad insisted that God's revelation in the Quran was not altogether new: the Quran reconfirmed God's revelation made to the prophets throughout human history and, in particular, the prophets in the tradition of Israel, among whom special mention is made of Adam, Eve, Noah, Moses, Jesus and Mary. Men and women in other religious and cultural traditions, when addressed by the divine voice, have also recognized the one and only God, Author of the universe, and the moral norms of human conduct. According to the Prophet, the previous revelations have not always been correctly interpreted. The Quran honours the biblical tradition of Jews and Christians, even if it claims that they have misinterpreted certain aspects of God's Word. The Quran confirms and corrects all previous divine revelations: it

presents itself as the final and definitive revelation and the
seal of the prophetic traditions.

According to the Prophet Muhammad, there is some-
thing blind, irrational and destructive in polytheism. The
belief in the plurality of gods contradicts human intelligence
and generates an ethic that is damaging to the human community. In Arabia, still subject to polytheistic beliefs and
practices, the Quranic revelation produced a cultural revolution, yet in parts of the world where prophets had already
made known the One God and His moral prescriptions,
the Quran presented itself as a reaffirmation of the ancient
wisdom in its final and definitive form. In His great mercy,
God has not been silent, God has not left Himself without
witnesses, God has spoken to the whole of humanity.

God's Word revealed by the prophets is able to convince
people because it is validated by their intelligence. Reflecting on their experience of life and on the world in which
they live, men and women are able to endorse that there
is one God, the Author of all that is, and a moral code,
written into their hearts, that corresponds to the revealed
ethos. Ramadan insists that there is no contradiction in
Islam between faith and reason. He mentions in particular
that Muhammad never appealed to miracles to persuade his
audience. Divine persuasion relies on human intelligence.
To the reflective person, the experience of being human and
situated in the universe gives witness of God's authorship.
Ramadan writes, "Nature is a book abounding in signs of its
essential link with the divine, this 'natural faith,' this 'faith
within nature,' that is chanted by the mountain and the

desert, the tree and the bird." He then adds this quotation from the Quran, "Art thou not aware that it is God whose limitless glory all creatures that are in the heavens and on earth extol, even the birds as they spread out their wings? Each of them knows indeed how to pray unto Him and to glorify Him, and God has full knowledge of all that they do."[52] Because divine self-revelation is taking place in the works of creation, Muslims refer to nature as the second sacred book, the first being the Quran.

The relationship between revelation, reason and nature is further clarified in the Quranic teaching of creation. That God is Creator means not only that human beings and their world are made by Him, but also and more especially that the entire created reality, humans as well as nature, bear the stamp of His creation. This means that their dependence on God is written into their being, that their origin in Him makes them witnesses of His power, and that their very essence orients them toward surrender to the divine will. This inner orientation toward God is referred to in the Quran as *fitra*, a word translated in various ways. Ramadan writes, "In the heart and consciousness of each individual there exist an essential and profound intuitive awareness and recognition of the presence of the Transcendent. Just as the sun, the clouds, the wind and the birds, and all the animals, express their natural submission, ... the human being has within it an almost instinctive longing for a dimension that is 'beyond.'"[53]

To shed light on this orientation or *fitra*, Ramadan uses a beautiful Quranic image: he writes that God has created humans by His breath and that this breath remains with them. The divine breath dwells in their hearts and guides their intelligence so that they are able to recognize the Creator and distinguish between good and evil. Because of the divine breath in them, people are able to acknowledge their need of God. Ramadan quotes the Quran: "Surrender your whole being as a true believer and in accordance with the *fitra*, the natural desire, which God gave to human beings when He created them."[54] Created by God, human beings in some way reflect their Creator: they give testimony of God's glory, and they are destined to mirror God's oneness, *tahwid*, by constituting a single covenant. Their *fitra* orients them to become witnesses of God and strive to become brothers and sisters in a single family.

Surrendering to God's will is the call addressed to all human beings, not only to Muslims enlightened by the Quran. Thanks to God's breath that dwells in their hearts, men and women everywhere are able to follow their *fitra* and become obedient to God's will. Their trusting surrender to God makes them Muslims: Muslims outside the *umma*, Muslims unbeknownst to themselves, Muslims destined to be with God in the age to come.

Theological anthropology

Ramadan offers his readers the interpretation of human existence according to the Muslim faith. He develops the theological anthropology implicit in the Quranic revelation. Human beings, created by God's breath as intelligent actors, are dependent on their Creator and oriented toward Him. If they are reflective, they will experience their need of God and discover signs of the Transcendent in the world and in their personal experience. If they are in touch with the depth of their heart, they bow down in worship before their Creator, become His witnesses and extend their solidarity to the worldwide human community.

With the entire Muslim tradition, Ramadan affirms the great mystery, transcending human understanding, that God is the omnipotent Creator and Lord of the universe and, at the same time, human beings are free agents capable of obeying or disobeying God's will. While they are steered towards God by their *fitra*, they are free to disregard the inner voice, lead a non-reflective existence and give in to their self-centredness. Humans are free to say yes or no to the divine voice. More than that, the Quran recognizes men and women as historical agents, vice-regents of God, summoned to build a just and peace-loving society: "It is God who has made you His vice-regents on earth."[55] In their effort they are sustained by the One God, *tahwid*, drawing humanity and nature toward a creative reconciliation in unity and peace.

We saw that Ramadan bases the universal message of Islam on the doctrine of creation and the stamp which the Creator's breath imprints on each human being. The same universal message is presented by another Muslim theologian, recalling that God is the eternal Light that shines into the lives of all human beings.[56] "God is the Light of the heaven and earth. His Light is like this: there is a niche, and in it a lamp, the lamp inside a glass, a glass like a glittering star, fuelled from a blessed olive tree from neither east nor west, whose oil gives light even when no fire touches it – light upon light – God guides whomever he will to His Light" (Quran 24:35).

Ramadan repeatedly assures the reader that the universal message of the Quran does not distract from the crucial importance of the Quran's particular message addressed to the Muslim community. Because the divine drama taking place in history and the cosmos is a largely hidden reality, the Quran communicates the divine revelation in a visible, palpable, concrete manner, providing ritual practices, moral norms and legal principles. In the *umma*, the Muslim community, the divine intention for the world becomes fully explicit and is realized in history. Muslims are grateful for *sharia*, the divine guidance for the holy life, because they are keenly aware of the fragile human condition. We shall study Ramadan's interpretation of *sharia* in the next chapter.

Still, Ramadan believes that his theological anthropology will please the Western Muslims whom he addresses. It allows them to look beyond their own community, recognize God's work in the pluralistic world, and engage in actions of solidarity with non-Muslim individuals and groups.

Comparing Muslim and Christian teaching

Christian readers are also impressed by Ramadan's theological anthropology. The teaching that all men and women who obey God's will are in fact Muslims – Muslims without knowing it – reminds the Christian reader of an analogous

Christian idea, implicit in the words of Jesus: "Anyone who does the will of my Father in heaven is my brother, sister and mother" (Mt 12:50, see also Lk 8:21). Wherever men and women do God's will, they belong to the family of Jesus. This implication was recognized by the early Church fathers. They attached great importance to the verses of the Prologue to John's gospel: "In the beginning was the Word, and the Word was with God and the Word was God ... and the Word was the real Light that gives light to everyone coming into the world" (John 1:1, 9). They interpreted this to mean that every human being is addressed by the Word of God: God's grace is offered universally. Wherever people say yes to this gift, they belong to the family of Jesus. This ancient teaching, largely neglected in the Church's history, assumed central importance in the writings of 20th-century Catholic theologians, in particular Henri de Lubac and Karl Rahner, and found formal expression in the teaching of the Second Vatican Council.[57] Here it was argued that God's Word, incarnate in Jesus, resounds in the whole of human history, addressing people wherever they are – through their experience of life and through the religious and cultural traditions to which they belong. God graciously summons people everywhere to recognize their selfishness and, trusting in the Voice that calls them, be converted to the love of neighbour and to solidarity with the weak. While this is the teaching of the Second Vatican Council, it has not yet been assimilated by all church-going Catholics, many of whom still hold an older teaching that there is no salvation outside the visible boundaries of the Church.

Both in Islam and in Catholicism, we conclude, a strong and well-grounded theological current affirms that the merciful God invites all human beings to do His will and enter into His blessedness. At the same time, there is a difference between Muslim and Catholic teaching. According to Ramadan, God's creation leaves upon human beings a stamp that leads them on their way to God. The created order here includes the grace that orients humans toward eternal life with God. By contrast, according to Catholic teaching, the created order has been disrupted by "original sin": pride and violence have turned the human world into a realm of injustice and inequality. Yet humans, now estranged from God, are not left in this condition: God decides to rescue them, extend them forgiveness, and grace them to become God's friends. In Muslim theology, grace is included in the order of creation, while in Catholic teaching grace is granted by a second gesture consequent upon creation. There are Catholic theologians, especially in the Franciscan tradition, who hold that God's creative and redemptive activity are intertwined and that, from the beginning, the creation of humans was accompanied by the grace of divine friendship, a position that comes closer to the theology of Tariq Ramadan.

Ramadan recognizes the difference between the Muslim and the Christian theologies of creation. He reminds his readers that the Quran does not share the Christian teaching of an original sin, in which humans are born and from which they will have to be saved. According to the Quran, creation itself is gracious: since God's breath remains in the men and women created by Him, they find mercy and forgiveness by returning to their origin. Muslims, Ramadan argues, embrace life confidently: they are not troubled – as Christians are – by a sin that has wounded human existence independently of personal fault.

Here, I think, Ramadan exaggerates a little. After all, he repeatedly reminds us that the human condition is such that every man and woman must wrestle against selfishness, pride and greed. Ramadan even speaks of "the natural human tendency to forget God."[58] While humans live out of the original gift and, returning to their *fitra*, are enabled to do God's holy will, they are also subject to an inclination to resist the divine will. That inclination must be wrestled against. It calls for a disciplined struggle, the great *jihad* in which all humans must engage. Muslims are grateful for God's revelation in the Quran, since this gives them precise directions. While Islam does not speak of an original sin, Ramadan's theology acknowledges the vulnerability of the human heart, oriented toward God and yet caught up in selfishness. Because of the ambiguity in their heart, humans can be their own worst enemy and enter upon a life that leads to eternal perdition. The good news of the Quran is that God addresses them, rescues them, sustains them in their struggle and helps them to surrender themselves to His will. God is here Saviour. While this teaching differs from the Christian doctrines of original sin and divine redemption, it has nonetheless a certain affinity with them.

Ramadan sees a another difference between the Muslim and the Christian understandings of the human condition.

Muslim thought, he holds, is not troubled by the dualisms that characterize the Christian theological tradition: the tensions between faith and reason, body and soul, individual and community, earthly life and life in the age to come. Reflective Muslims, Ramadan tells us, marvel at the unifying forces present in their lives and the world to which they belong. The Oneness of God, *tahwid*, is mirrored in the created order, producing an inner coherence among its many parts and drawing them into ever greater unity. According to Ramadan, Islamic thought perceives harmony between faith and reason; it recognizes the unity of persons, refusing to assign inferiority to the bodily parts; it sees no conflict between personal life and the common good; and it balances the attachment to earthly life and the desire for the world to come. Islam inspires the search for the middle, the avoidance of one-sidedness, the balance among human capacities.

This is a theme I also find in other Muslim thinkers of *al-nahda*. Said Nursi, the influential Sufi thinker of Turkey who died in 1964, presented Islam as "the middle way," fostering peace, balance, justice and moderation, radically incompatible with fanaticism of any kind.[59] Studying the work of Fethullah Gülen, who followed Nursi's lead, I found that the former also finds harmony between the mystical and the legal dimensions of Islam, between the body's and the soul's well-being, between feelings and human reason, between the individual and the community, between justice and mercy, and between concern for this world and the longing for the age to come.[60]

Overcoming the dualities of human existence may well characterize Islam interpreted by the renewal movement. Yet this is not necessarily true for the other currents of Islam. We shall see in chapter 4 that some of them entertain a dualistic perception of the world, divided between the Islamic abode and the abode of hostility;[61] some even project the dualism between insiders and outsiders onto their own community by assigning men and women to different realms.

As there are distinct currents in Islam, so there are in Christianity. Not all theological currents in Christianity are bearers of the dualisms mentioned by Ramadan. In contemporary Christian thought, influenced by feminist thought, liberation theology and ecological concern, efforts are being made to overcome dualistic thinking and recognize the multi-dimensional character of the one historical reality.

The preceding paragraphs show that, because of the internal pluralism present in every religion, it is difficult to make general statements about a religion and even more difficult to make comparisons between different religions. What may be more productive, I am prepared to argue, is to focus on currents in different religions that enjoy an affinity or share a perspective. This is in fact my approach to the study of Ramadan's theology. His critical openness to modernity represents a current in Islam that has an affinity with contemporary Catholic theology.

Two Christian questions

I wish to raise two Christian questions. Because the practice of *sharia* demands the observance of a set of rituals and
regulations, Christians wonder how Muslims understand
their good works. Do Muslims think that they can earn their
entry into heaven by their own effort? Does the observance
of *sharia* merit life eternal? Or do they recognize a divine
prompting in their good works and hence thank God for
their fidelity? Christians have regarded this as an important
question. The idea of meriting salvation by one's own effort
or acquiring holiness by an effort of the will was condemned
as a heresy in the fifth century. It was deemed contrary to
the teaching of St. Paul. The heretical teaching was called
Pelagianism after Pelagius, a teacher of asceticism who
held that humans could enter into friendship with God by
their own moral effort. This was condemned in 418 by the
Council of Carthage IV and again in 521 by the Council
of Orange II. The conciliar teaching reminded the faithful
of Christ's words: "Without me you can do nothing" (Jn
15:5). It declared that faith, hope and love were unmerited
divine gifts and that the good deeds that will be rewarded
in the age to come are the fruit of divine grace acting in
the human heart. Humans are prompted to be good by a
gratuitous divine initiative. While this is the Church's official teaching, the sermons preached in parishes are often
purely moralistic, urging people to rely on their willpower
to do good.

Christians wonder whether Muslims are "Pelagians" – i.e., whether they think that the observance of *sharia* merits eternal life. Tariq Ramadan's theology gives a clear answer to this question. Since the breath of God remains in the men and women created by Him, they are urged and enabled to be good by an original gift, a divinely imprinted inclination, that prompts them to worship God and to do God's will. According to Ramadan's theology, Muslims are not Pelagians: their freedom to say an unreserved yes to God is produced by their *fitra*, their original gift, addressed by the Quranic revelation. Their faith, their dedication and their daily practice are God's gift to them.

The second Christian question is a modern one. Christian theologians were greatly challenged by Immanuel Kant's distinction between heteronomy and autonomy. Kant argued that an ethics imposed upon humans by a higher authority, even if this authority be divine, is damaging to them: it locks them into a state of immaturity and prevents them from achieving their autonomy, i.e., the capacity to define the good by their own intelligence. Humans suffer heteronomy, Kant agued, if they are subject to the rule of another.

This distinction prompted Christian theologians to ask themselves whether Christian morality imposes heteronomy on believers, or whether it encourages believers to formulate their ethical vision according to a principle internal to them. Do believers, in doing good, submit themselves to the rule of Another? Or is the goodness they seek the fulfillment of their natural inclination?

Many Christians interpret the good life as the observance of God's commandments. They are not bothered by the accusation of heteronomy. Yet Christian theologians have often tried to show that the holy life corresponds to the deepest desire of the human heart. St. Augustine believed that God utters His Word in two ways: externally, through the Bible and the Church's preaching, and internally, through the Spirit touching the human heart. He therefore held that God's commandments are not imposed on a reluctant believer; they are received, rather, as the confirmation of what the heart touched by the Spirit yearns for. Catholic theologians in the Thomistic tradition argue that the life of virtue is the fulfillment of people's natural desire: responding to God's grace and striving for holiness, people realize their full human potential and become truly themselves. Here God is not seen as imposing ethical norms from above, but rather as aiding humans to discover the way that leads to the fulfilment of their nature. For Thomists, Christians do not suffer heteronomy; instead, they enjoy graced autonomy.

Not unrelated to these theologies are the proposals of 20th-century Catholic and Protestant theologians – for instance, Karl Rahner and Paul Tillich – who argue that uttered in the process of human self-realization is a gracious divine summons. For this reason, the proclamation of the Gospel does not subject humans to heteronomy, but rather makes explicit the hidden graciousness operative in their lives. While Christian ethics is not heteronomous, neither Rahner nor Tillich want to say that it is autonomous: using this expression would seem to deny any link between ethics and the divine. Paul Tillich created a new term: humans, he argued, are neither heteronomous nor autonomous, they are instead "theonomous" – guided by the divine light in their intelligence.

Ramadan also offers a theological interpretation of human life to show that Muslim ethics does not subject believers to heteronomy. *Sharia* is revealed by God to remind humans of the original gift they received in creation: namely, the summons to give witness to their Creator and to live in covenant with all human beings. It follows that Muslims who observe the divinely given rites and regulations are not subjecting themselves to a law externally imposed on them, but acting in fidelity to what is deepest in their heart.

Ramadan's theology gives a clear answer to the question of whether an action is good because it is commanded by God, or whether God commands it because it is good. According to the universal message of Islam, God has created an ordered universe in which the good has an objective reality – and God commands that this good be done. God is not a sovereign ruler who imposes His rule in arbitrary fashion. In giving His commands, God is faithful to Himself and His work of creation.[62]

Ecology and science

Ramadan's emphasis on the *fitra*, the orienting impulse implicit in creation, has marked not only his theological anthropology but also his theology of the natural world.

Minerals, plants and animals are internally oriented toward
obedience to God's will; in their very being they worship
their Creator. We read in the Quran, "The sun and the
moon follow courses exactly computed; the herbs and the
trees – both, alike, bow in adoration; the firmament He has
raised high" (Quran 55:5-7). The cosmos itself is Muslim,
surrendered to God's will.

Ramadan only hints that this understanding of nature
is the foundation for a theology of the environment. Even
though he does not deal specifically with the ecological
crisis, I wish to pursue the topic since it has produced a
lively debate among Muslim thinkers.

The substantial volume *Islam and Ecology*[63] offers a series
of essays, most of them written by Muslim scholars, that
find in the Quran resources for a theology of the natural
world and for guidance in the present ecological crisis. It is
not surprising, these scholars write, that as a desert-dweller
the Prophet recognized the delicate natural balance that
assures the survival of humans, animals and plants. The
authors of these essays agree that the Quran summons believers to respect and protect the natural environment. They
acknowledge the theological point made by Ramadan that
the *fitra*, the inner orientation of creation, makes all beings,
animate and inanimate, worshippers of God. The authors
also recognize that God has appointed humans as vice-
regents or stewards of the natural world, assigning them
the responsibility for taking care of the environment and
protecting it against exploitation and ruin. Since the poor
are more vulnerable than the rich to ecological disasters,

the authors of this volume tend to link their theology of
the environment to considerations of social justice. They
offer a reading of the Quran that demands both respect for
nature and a commitment to social justice – an emphasis
shared, as we shall see, by Tariq Ramadan.

The world of scholars and public opinion woke up to
the threat to the natural environment only a few decades
ago. It is instructive to compare the Christian and the Muslim reaction to this disturbing discovery. Rachel Carson's
The Silent Spring, published in 1962, is often regarded as the
starting point for a new ecological awareness.[64] In 1967,
Lynn White published the article "On the Historical Roots
of Our Ecological Crisis."[65] In that article, he blamed the
biblical tradition for orienting Western culture toward the
control and exploitation of nature and an unlimited striving
for progress – an orientation that has produced the present
life-destroying environmental crisis. Recalling God's commandment to humans "to subdue the earth and be masters
of the fish of the sea, the birds of heaven and all the living
creatures that move on earth" (Gen 1:28), White argued
that the Bible looks upon the natural world as a force to
be mastered, an object to be used and a resource to be
exploited.

The replies to White's article constitute an extensive
theological literature. Many biblical scholars disagree with
White's interpretation: the divine commandment to subdue
the earth, they argue, was addressed to a peasant people that
tilled the ground and tamed animals to help them in their
labour. The threat to the environment, theologians have

argued, arrived only with the advent of industrialization. Still, awakened to the ongoing damage to the environment, Christian scholars admitted that they had failed to recognize this danger. Rereading the Scriptures, they now found resources for an ecological theology that called for the protection of the natural environment.

Less well known is that a year prior to Lynn White's article, in 1966, a young Muslim philosopher, Seyyed Hossein Nasr, gave a set of learned lectures in Chicago on the emerging environmental crisis that offered an analysis of the grave situation from a Muslim theological perspective. These lectures were published two years later as *The Encounter of Man and Nature: The Spiritual Crisis of Modern Man*.[66] In it Nasr denounced modern Western science as the culprit of the ecological crisis.

Who was the Muslim scholar disturbed at such an early date by the destruction of the natural environment? Hossein Nasr, born in Iran, was sent to the United States to study the sciences, especially physics. While a student at the Massachusetts Institute of Technology, he heard a lecture by Bertrand Russell in which the British scientist declared that the sciences, important as they are, have nothing to say about the meaning of life. After this lecture, Hossein Nasr tells us, he could not sleep all night. As a believing Muslim, he held that knowledge that did not reveal the meaning of existence was not knowledge at all. He therefore decided to interrupt his scientific studies and turn to the history of the sciences – the Islamic and the Western sciences. While he studied for his doctorate at Harvard University, he observed that the building of express highways through and around the city of Boston damaged the countryside and destroyed the natural environment. It was this shock and this sadness that made him prepare the 1966 lectures in Chicago on the emerging ecological crisis in the light of Islamic faith.

According to this faith, the unity and unicity of God (*tahwid*) is mirrored in all of God's creation, in the unity of the human family, the unity of the cosmos, and the human striving, through knowledge and action, to create a unifying balance between culture and nature. According to Nasr, Western science violates this orientation towards unity. Western science turns nature into a series of objects, each distinct from the other and isolated from the totality – a series of objects that can be controlled and manipulated by the powerful in the pursuit of their selfish desires. According to Nasr, Western science detaches humans from the God who sustains them and offers them wisdom: it fosters the secularization of culture. In addition, by disrupting the cosmic order, Western science fosters the destruction of the natural environment. What is needed, according to Nasr, is the spiritual conversion of Western civilization to the Creator and Sustainer of the universe.

Nasr offered a passionate argument that Muslims should return to their own tradition of science and develop it in accordance with the spirit of Islam. He wanted Muslims to promote the islamization of knowledge. He disagreed with the Muslim thinkers of the renewal movement, *al-nahda* – Ramadan's theological home – because they have criticized the resistance of Muslims to Western science and

persuaded them to study these sciences and make use of
them in the promotion of their own oriental cultures. Nasr
believes that these reformers are naive in their hope that the
destructive impact of the sciences can be overcome if the
application of the sciences is guided by ethical principles
in keeping with God's will.

Many Muslim thinkers disagree with Nasr: they do not
believe that the study of modern science produces necessarily the secularization of culture. The Turkish theologian
Fethullah Gülen, echoing the position of Said Nursi, argues
that believing Muslims doing scientific research on the
laws of nature are deeply moved by the marvels of God's
wisdom and power: "The scientific study of heat and light,
of plants and animals, of human bodies and cosmic events
reveals the traces and the works of the divine Creator."[67]
Scientists, Gülen holds, glorify God in a particular manner.
The social movement inspired by Gülen has created many
schools in Turkey and other countries that put great emphasis on the study of science. Interviews with the teachers at
these institutions reveal that they attach religious meaning
to their work and encounter the wonders of God in their
courses on science.[68]

Since Said Nursi and, after him, Fethullah Gülen live in a
believing Muslim environment, they hold that the spiritual
experience of scientific research can be communicated to
students at schools and universities. Living in the West,
Tariq Ramadan is unable to promise with Nursi and Gülen
that the study of science offers religious experiences, nor
does he agree with Nasr that the Western sciences should

be abandoned in favour of Islamic sciences yet to be articulated. Neither does he accept Nasr's accusation that he naively trusts in the ability of Western society to provide ethical guidelines for the development and application of the sciences.

If I read Ramadan correctly, he has sympathy for the Muslim philosopher Mohammed Taleb's critique of the practice of Western science. Taleb questions these sciences on the basis of a Western intellectual tradition that, he believes, has an affinity with Muslim thought.[69] It is not science itself that causes the violation of nature and "the disenchantment of the world" – an expression of Max Weber's, taken from the poet Friedrich Schiller – the fault lies rather with the orientation of scientific research and its application, steered by the capitalist economy and driven by the maximization of profit and the military defence of its interests. The Frankfurt School, which Taleb likes to quote, denounces the domination of instrumental reason – the dominant techno-scientific utilitarianism detached from any ethical norms – as the cause reducing the world to a series of objects to be manipulated and, if possible, turned into commodities. Taleb does not call upon society to give up science; what he calls for, following the Frankfurt School, is the transmutation of capitalism, the decentering of techno-scientific reason, and the retrieval of ethical reason to protect the *humanum* and the natural world.

The ecological imperative belongs to what Ramadan calls Islam's universal message.

4

Sharia: The Muslim Way of Life

The Quran's *universal* message confirms and clarifies all previous divine revelations as well as the intuition of thoughtful people reflecting on the yearning of their hearts and the world around them. The Quran's *particular* message is addressed to Muslims, initiating them into the way of life pleasing to God. This is the *sharia*, the set of exhortations, principles, rituals and laws that defines the worship of God and the holy life in community, thus confirming the inner orientation of humans toward their Creator. Since humans easily forget God and forget about God, *sharia* reminds them of their origin and their destiny in God. According to Tariq Ramadan, Muslims rejoice in the gift of *sharia*.

Ramadan is aware at the same time that the very word *sharia* suggests to non-Muslims living in the West a totally outmoded legal system that curtails the free development of Muslims, subjects women to the control of men, and imposes the most cruel punishments on those who violate the law. Ramadan regards it as his task as a theologian to clarify the notion of *sharia* and reveal its life-giving power.

He recognizes that after the early period of the rightly guided caliphs, the Quran was interpreted by the *ulama*, who derived from the revealed text rules and regulations to assure that the *umma*, the believing community, remained faithful to God's revelation. These *ulama*, Ramadan writes, were jurists, not theologians. Their main concern was the right ordering of the community in accordance to God's will.

The Quran read by jurists

Today, Muslim scholars recognize that verses of the Quran that deal with legal issues are very few – less than 5 per cent of the total.[70] The greater part of the Quran proclaims the uniqueness of the One God, offers divine praises, reveals the mission of the Prophet, recalls previous divine revelations, records God's promises for this life and the next, lauds divine mercy, exhorts believers to lead a virtuous life and threatens those who do evil. On the Arabian peninsula, Islam was at the outset a new faith and a new ethos – a radically new way of life offered to the tribes, which were in conflict with one another, imprisoned in polytheistic beliefs and practices. This new life was sustained by the five pillars of Islam, i) the public witness, ii) the daily prayers, iii) the alms for the poor, iv) the specified fasts, and v) the holy pilgrimage. The later part of the Quran, revealed in Medina when the *umma* sought to organize itself as a stable society, offers regulations regarding social issues such as marriage, commerce, peace-making and war. Yet even these verses deal for the greater part with general principles, such as respect, solidarity, justice and kindness, rather than offering detailed laws.

Under the Umayyad Dynasty (661–750), as we saw in chapter 2, the caliphs did not see themselves as the guardians of the faith. This task was assumed by the *ulama*, the scholars, the jurists, whose passionate concern was the fidelity of the community to God's revelation. They focused on the Quranic passages that dealt with social issues, deriving from them the rules and laws destined to guide the community and reply to practical questions that emerged in it. These scholars began what came to be called the Islamic sciences. As we saw in chapter 2, this research was carried on in renowned schools of Islamic law, some of which have retained their authority to this day.

These jurists tended to adopt a purely juridical understanding of *sharia*, while, Ramadan insists, *sharia* refers to the Muslim way of life: Muslims practise *sharia* when they give witness to God, say their prayers, offer alms and observe the fast. They practice *sharia* when they worship God and follow the Islamic ethos. *Sharia* includes rules and laws, yet it refers to a wider reality, the entire path that leads to God. Ramadan regrets that the dominant juridical tradition has persuaded many Muslims to think of *sharia* in purely juridical terms and thus believe that they are faithful to Islam when they observe all the rules. Ramadan reminds them that observance is an expression of faith only when it is part of a life surrendered to God.

How does Ramadan relate himself to the juridical tradition in Islam? This is the difficult question that I will try to
answer in this chapter.

The first thing to remember is that Ramadan sees himself
as belonging to *Salafi* reformism, i.e., the Islamic renewal
movement (*al-nahda*) started by al-Afghani at the end of
the nineteenth century. These reformers were eager "to
bypass the boundaries marked out by the juridical schools
in order to rediscover the pristine energy of an unmediated
reading of the Quran and the Sunna."[71] We saw in chapter
2 that the thinkers of the *al-nahda* wanted to return to the
Islam practised by the Prophet and his Companions. These
thinkers thought that Islam was open to reason and common
sense and capable of responding creatively to new historical
challenges. We also saw in chapter 2 that the *Salafi* traditionalists – the literalists, as I called them – also wanted to
bypass the schools of law and return to the Quran. The great
difference between the reformers and the literalists is that
the former read the Quranic texts by taking into account
their historical context and the intention behind the text,
while the latter adopt a literalist reading.

Hermeneutics

Ramadan insists on the key difference between his own
reformist approach and the fundamentalist prejudice of the
literalists. The reformist approach, he explains, reads the
Quran by taking into account the context of the verses and
the intention implicit in them.[72] What is the source of this
hermeneutical principle? He shows that this is the way the

Quranic revelation was interpreted by the Prophet and his Companions. Ramadan mentions in particular the ruling of Caliph Umar that the punishment for stealing, demanded by the Quran, should not be applied during the famine, when some people had to steal in order to survive.[73] Ramadan suggests that the same principle was subsequently applied by certain *ulama* of the classical Islamic juridical schools.

I am not fully convinced by this suggestion. Taking into account the context and the intention behind the text limits the meaning of a passage, while the traditional jurists, using the principle of analogy, tended to expand this meaning. Instead of restricting the relevance of the text to certain clearly defined situations, the *ulama* tended to extend its binding power to increasingly wider situations. Thus the Prophet's objection to pictures of humans and animals, fearing a return to polytheistic practices, was expanded by the *ulama* to become a condemnation of all paintings and sculptures representing living things. If the *ulama* had taken into account the context of these texts and the intention behind them, they would have limited the Prophet's objections to situations where believers are surrounded by a polytheistic culture and tempted by idolatry. I am not persuaded, therefore, that Ramadan's hermeneutic principle was fully applied by the Islamic schools of law. He gives evidence that it was applied in a spontaneous manner, following good common sense, by the Prophets and his Companions, yet making use of it as a formal principle to be applied consistently and systematically is, I suspect, an innovation.

In the Catholic tradition, the application of this hermeneutical principle to the interpretation of Scripture was
permitted only fairly recently. In the nineteenth century, the
Vatican forbade biblical scholars to interpret the meaning
of Scripture by taking into account the historical context
of the passage and the intention of its author. This historical critical method was thought to undermine the universal
relevance of God's Word. It was only in 1943 that Pius XII,
in his encyclical *Divino afflante Spiritu*, gave biblical scholars
the permission to make a wise use of the new method of
interpretation. At present, this method of interpretation
is recommended in the Catholic Catechism. "In order to
discover the sacred authors' intention, the reader must take
into account the conditions of their time and culture, the
literary genres in use at that time, and the modes of feeling, speaking and narrating then current. For ... truth is
differently presented and expressed in the various types of
historical writing, in prophetical and poetical texts, and in
other forms of literary expression."[74]

Ramadan's hermeneutical principle is applied by many
contemporary Muslim scholars. I wish to give a few examples to show how important this approach is and how it
differs from literalism.

The Quranic verse "Slay them wherever you find them"
(2:191) could be read to mean that Muslims should kill
non-Muslims wherever they find them.[75] A literalist reading of this verse is misleading and dangerous. In actual fact,
the only situation in which the Quran allows Muslims to
fight is in self-defence or in defending the oppressed who

are calling for help. In the present verse, "them" refers to fighters from Mecca who are attacking the Muslim community. The verse gave permission to the Prophet and his followers to fight the Meccan aggressors. Yet since Mecca was a sanctuary in which killing was forbidden, including the killing of animals, the besieged Muslims asked themselves whether they could fight the Meccan attackers only outside the city or also within it. The present verse replies to this question by saying, "wherever you find them," i.e., outside and inside the city.

Another example of taking account of the context and the author's intention is the interpretation offered by contemporary Muslims regarding the Islamic prohibition of making pictures of human beings and animals. Celebrating the Oneness of God and denouncing polytheistic practices, the Quran warned against all forms of idolatry (42: -11; 21:54-55). In subsequent generations, this warning, plus a number of other texts, was interpreted as a prohibition of pictures and statues of humans and animals. This interpretation was confirmed by remarks of the Prophet recorded in the Sunna, in which he objected to the picture of Abraham and Ishmael and, at another occasion, to the picture of a dog decorating a cushion.[76] Yet with the arrival of photography and movies, many Muslim scholars had second thoughts. They argued that the Quranic prohibition was uttered in a context where Muslims were still vulnerable to idolatrous practices, but that at present the Oneness of God has been so profoundly assimilated by the Muslim community that the enjoyment of photographs and films offered no temptation of idolatry. Gradually, the *ulama* changed their teaching: they allowed the making of photographic pictures and prohibited only pictorial representations of the Prophet, fearing that the veneration Muslims have for him could turn into worship. What remains of the original prohibitions is the divine request that Muslims choose worthy topics in their pictorial arts.[77]

Here is another example. Ramadan reports an interpretation of the Quranic verses on polygamy proposed by Muhammad Abduh, the disciple and colleague of al-Afghani.[78] In Sura 4:2, the Prophet allows Muslim men to marry up to four wives, a permission that has been regarded for centuries as a sacred right. The renewal movement in critical dialogue with modernity was embarrassed by this permission, because it implied the subordination of women, chided in other passages in the Quran. To the permission of polygamy, it was noted, the Prophet had added this sentence: "If you fear that you cannot be equitable to them, then marry only one" (4:3). Mohammad Abduh argued that since polygamy was universally practised in Arabia, the Prophet felt that he could not abolish it altogether, but that by adding the demand of being equally just to all the wives, he revealed his true intention. Since to be equitable to several wives is practically impossible, he hinted that the Muslim practice would eventually be monogamous.

In defence of authority

Since Ramadan as a Salafi reformist wants Muslims to transcend the regulations of the Islamic schools of law "to

rediscover the pristine energy of an unmediated reading of
the Quran," the reader may think that he is asking Muslims
to read the Quran for themselves and, conscious of their
own historical situation, find in its passages guidance for
the direction of their lives. Yet Ramadan does not do this:
he opposes private interpretation. Only the *ulama*, scholars
trained in the Islamic sciences, have the competence to
interpret the Quran. The reader is surprised by Ramadan's
defence of authority. Ramadan wants to bypass the regulations of the Islamic schools of law and at the same time – if
I understand him correctly – interpret the Quran according
to principles recognized by the Islamic sciences.

Before further exploring Ramadan's defence of authority,
I wish to mention a different approach taken by another
well-known Muslim reformist theologian. Farid Esack, a
scholar born in South Africa who received his religious
academic education in Pakistan and Britain, depicts in his
writings the experience of young Muslims living under the
apartheid regime of South Africa. They sought an answer
to the burning question of how God wanted them to act
in their historical situation.[79] Esack reports that the *ulama*
in South Africa did not deal with this issue. They interpreted the Quran following the guidance of a particular
Islamic school of law without any reference to the injustice
inflicted upon the non-white population of the country.
Esack recounts how he and his friends went directly to the
Quran and how amazed they were by the many passages
that demanded social justice, condemned conditions of
oppression, and encouraged them to wrestle against dis-

crimination and domination. The young Muslims believed they were obedient to God's revelation when they actively joined the struggle against apartheid and worked together with activists of other backgrounds, religious and secular. Reading the Quran daily, they felt supported by God in their struggle. Esack recognizes here a parallel to Christian liberation theology, which proposes that the struggle for social justice is blessed and supported by Jesus, who came to bring sight to the blind, good news to the poor, release to prisoners and freedom to the oppressed (Lk 4:18).

At the same time, Esack raises a serious difficulty. He tells us that among the young Muslim anti-apartheid activists, some looked forward to the creation of pluralistic and democratic South Africa, while others regarded the present struggle as the first step toward the creation of an Islamic state. Using Ramadan's vocabulary, some of these activists were *Salafi* reformists, while others were politicized *Salafi* literalists. The events reported by Farid Esack help us to understand why Tariq Ramadan discourages private interpretation and defends the teaching authority of the *ulama*.

Ramadan wants to transcend the limitations imposed by the Islamic schools of law and engage in a fresh reading of the Quran, yet in doing so, he wishes to follow hermeneutical principles that are respected by these schools. He wants the new insights he seeks to be in continuity with the Islamic tradition. We shall see in another chapter that Ramadan's defence of authority has been criticized by liberal Muslim scholars who believe that making Islam relevant for the present age demands a break with tradition. In reply to them, Ramadan offers pastoral reasons for his commitment to remain within the tradition.

Ramadan addresses himself principally to Muslims living in Europe and in the Americas, most of whom have been brought up in a largely unreflective Islam defined in the distant past. He has called this "scholastic traditionalism." Vast numbers of these Muslims experience an inner conflict: they feel that their Islam does not offer them guidance in their present situation, and at the same time they mistrust innovative interpretations that depart from their tradition. Ramadan wants to convince them that their tradition offers principles that permit a rereading of the sacred texts, allowing Muslims to find in them the wisdom relevant to their situation. He wants to persuade them that fidelity to their religious inheritance does not prevent them from becoming fully Westerners, i.e., active and responsible citizens of their society. Because the rereading of the Quran must conform to the hermeneutical rules sanctified by the Islamic schools of law, it must be done by the *ulama*, scholars who are trained in the Islamic sciences.

Ramadan defends the authority of the *ulama* because he regards the reading of the Quran offered by the literalists and, more especially, by the politicized literalists as arbitrary and irresponsible. Literalists read the Quran by lifting passages out of their historical context: they propose that the lifestyle of the seventh-century Muslim community should be the model for faithful living today. Literalist Muslims in the West condemn themselves to live on the margins of society. Since they have their own *ulama* who bless their sectarian interpretation, Ramadan offers arguments based on tradition to persuade Muslims not to withdraw from society, but in the name of their faith to become citizens of society in the full sense.

Ramadan adopts a position deemed conservative by some because he disagrees with the tendency of liberals to rely uncritically on contemporary rationality. The important liberal Muslim thinkers tend to be university professors who do not share Ramadan's pastoral concern that ordinary Muslims will be able to recognize in the renewal of Islam the religion they have inherited and love. Ramadan is also critical of liberal interpretations of Islam adopted by governments of Muslim countries in order to engage in financial dealings and capitalist projects at odds with Islamic law and, worse, to dispense themselves from the Quranic obligation to serve their people, listen to their voice and foster their education. Ramadan insists that dictatorship and oppression are violations of *sharia*.

These are the reasons why this innovative theologian insists that the return to the Quran for inspiration may not set aside the reference to the Islamic sciences. Interpretation must therefore be done by an *ulama*, a trained scholar. That is why Ramadan decided to begin his book *To Be a European Muslim* with chapters on the Islamic sciences and the rules for extracting laws (*fiqh*) from the Quran and the Sunna. He wants to demonstrate both the freedom that the Islamic tradition allows and the need for disciplined scholarship to defend it.

Interpreting sharia

It is not my intention to present the detailed analysis of the sciences of *fiqh* that Ramadan offers his readers. In his introductory explanation, he speaks of three Islamic sciences that allow Muslim jurists to be faithful to the Quranic revelation and, at the same time, remain open to new developments. The *first* science provides rules and methodologies for extracting from the Quran and the Sunna the universal principles of *sharia* that guide the codification of Islamic law (*fiqh*). This law deals with two distinct fields: a) with issues related to worship and b) issues related to social affairs. The *second* science is related to worship: it applies the universal principles to the treatment of God's Oneness, the divine names and properties, the prayers of adoration and the believers' intimate relationship to God. These rules are permanent: they are applied universally throughout time. The *third* science is related to social affairs: it applies the universal principles to concrete matters such as marriage, customs, trade, self-defence and penal codes – matters that require constant reflection and adaptation to changing circumstances. The second science deals with what is unchanging in the practice of Islam, and the third science deals with what is changeable in this practice. The three sciences together show that perfect fidelity to the universal principles of *sharia* goes hand in hand with the freedom to act responsibly in the changing concrete situations of history.

Permanent and ever unchanging in Islam is the witness of faith: "I testify that there is no god but Allah and that

Muhammad is His Prophet." Permanent and unchanging are the remaining four pillars of Islam (prayer, alms, fasting and pilgrimage) and a few concrete prescriptions related mainly to the worship of God. Permanent and ever unchanging are the revealed truths about God and God's creation, the universal human virtues such as humility, piety, justice and compassion, and the universal principles of *sharia*. What must change are the applications of these principles in different historical contexts.

To assure that these changes are in conformity with God's revealed will, they have to be worked out by following rules that have been sanctified by the tradition. For this reason, interpreting *sharia* can be done only by a trained Islamic scholar. Ramadan offers a set of the rules that guide the interpretation (*ijtihad*) of the law. I wish to mention three of these rules in particular.

One set of rules is referred to as "permissibility." This encourages Muslims to be open to the world, encounter new cultures and appreciate new experiences. In Islam, cherishing the earthly life is permitted: the hope for the promised life in heaven does not lead to an otherworldly attitude. This openness to the whole of life is symbolized in the story of creation, where Adam and Eve are invited to eat from the different fruits in the garden, except one, "lest you become wrongdoers."[80] There are limits to permissibility, but they are few. "That which is lawful is plain, says the Prophet, and that which is unlawful is plain, and between the two are doubtful matters about which not many people know."[81] The *ulama* tried to clarify these matters. The Quran defines few obligations (*wajib*) and few prohibitions (*haram*). In the wide field of action between these, the *ulama* distinguish between actions that are "preferable," "allowed" and "reprehensible." According to the *ulama*, there is a radical opposition between *haram* (the prohibited) and *halal* (the permitted, in the widest meaning). *Halal* includes the few obligations (*wajib*) and actions that are "preferable" and "allowed" and even those that are "reprehensible." Ramadan argues that this range of permissibility, including entry into ambiguous areas, encourages Muslims to be venturesome.

The rules of permissibility are used by Ramadan to show that Islam is not locked into the culture in which it was revealed, but is able to move into other cultures, transform them and be transformed by them. He argues that Islam should be able to thrive in modern Western societies. How this can take place we shall see in the next chapter. Yet while Ramadan recognizes that Islam has many cultural faces, he insists that Islam is one. The many cultural incarnations of Islam do not produce several Islams; they all celebrate a single Islam, divinely revealed as the authentic religion. Ramadan assures his Muslim readers that by living as Westerners and following a way of life different from that of their parents or grandparents in the Orient, they continue to practise the identical Islam.

Another rule of interpretation (*ijtihad*) invokes the divine intention expressed in *sharia*. The pillars of Islam, the guidance to the universal virtues, and the legal prescriptions are intended by God to help believers worship their Creator, lead holy lives and constitute a just and peaceful society.

Confronted with questions raised in a new historical context, for which the sacred texts do not offer a direct reply, the *ulama* must find answers in keeping with the *sharia*. They may rely on analogies to actions approved in these sacred texts. If the sacred texts are silent on the issue, they may propose an answer to the problem by taking into account the intention of *sharia*, making society stable in justice and peace before God.

Ramadan used this rule to explain his position during the debate in the Canadian province of Ontario, where a Muslim association had asked the provincial government to allow the setting up of Islamic courts of arbitration dealing with business and family matters. Since the Arbitration Act of 1991 had permitted the creation of independent religious arbitration courts in Ontario, Catholics and Jews had occasionally used them to settle their internal conflicts.[82] Yet the demand made by Muslims provoked a vehement debate not only among the citizens of Ontario, but in the whole of Canada and even beyond. While the study commission set up by the government recommended that the demand be granted, the Canadian Muslim community was deeply divided over the issue. The Canadian Council of Muslim Women and other women's organizations strongly opposed the institution of independent religious courts. Tariq Ramadan, a frequent visitor to Canada, joined the debate: he spoke against the creation of Islamic courts. He argued that what *sharia* intends is the promotion of a just and peaceful society. For this reason, *sharia* obliges Muslims to obey the laws of the land in which they live: they may protest against a law only if it violates Islamic regulations. Ramadan argued that the present law of Ontario offered sound protection for families and people in business and thus merited the respect of Muslims living in Ontario: they had no need of independent courts.

A third rule of interpretation (*ijtihad*) of Islamic law (*fiqh*) on issues on which the sacred texts are unclear or silent is reference to the common good (*maslaha*). The traditional jurists, Ramadan reports, have sometimes offered bold interpretations of *sharia* regarding issues of urgent importance for the well-being of the community. Ramadan makes use of this rule when he tells Muslims living in the West that *sharia* demands that they become responsible citizens willing to contribute to the common good of society. As we shall see in the next chapter, Ramadan urges Western Muslims not to think of themselves as minorities whose concern is limited to the well-being of their religious community; he wants them to think of themselves as citizens in the full sense and to promote justice and peace in society in accordance with Islamic universal principles.

As we saw in chapter 2, Ramadan follows the Muslim historians who claim that between 1258 and 1870, Islam lost its creativity and experienced stagnation and decline. One reason for this was a decision made by some *umala* in the tenth century that was eventually accepted by all of them. Seeing that Islam was practised in many different cultures in regions from Andalusia to China, the *ulama* were increasingly afraid that encouraging creative developments would lead to infidelity to the Quranic revelation. They decreed therefore that "the gates of *ijtihad* " were now closed. Muslims were no longer allowed to respond creatively to new historical challenges. Muslim communities continued to be ruled by juridical decisions made centuries earlier by the classical Islamic schools of law. It was the renewal movement (*al nahda*) started by al-Afghani at the end of the nineteenth century that opened the gates of *ijtihad* and demonstrated the vitality and resourcefulness of Islam.

We saw that Ramadan's reading of the Quran and the Sunna promises great freedom. At the same time, we also learned that he disallows the private interpretation of the sacred texts and defends the authority of the *ulama*. To remain faithful to God's revelation in the West, the Muslim community is in need of declarations (*fatwa*) of properly trained scholars that offer authoritative interpretations of *sharia*. At present, these scholars are not in agreement; they offer declarations that contradict one another. In this situation, individual Muslims have the right to choose and follow the *fatwa* that is closest to their personal conscience. Ramadan believes that Islam would flourish in the West and reveal its creativity if the *ulama* in the West were in conversation with one another and arrived at common conclusions. We shall see in the next chapter that efforts in this direction have been made.

The Islamic corporal punishments

In his books addressed to Western Muslims, Ramadan does not raise the question of the Islamic punishments. In the West, Muslims are subject to the criminal law of the society in which they live. Yet Ramadan realizes that Westerners are profoundly shocked by the fixed corporal punishments (*hudud*) of certain crimes, such as public flogging, amputation of hands and execution by stoning. These practices, while sanctioned in the Quran and more especially the Sunna, embarrass Western Muslims whose sensibilities have been affected by the culture in which they live.

These cruel physical punishments were instituted at a time when the prison system, invented in modern times, did not exist. The accused were kept incarcerated only until their trial, after which, if found guilty, they were executed or sent home bleeding or maimed. In subsequent centuries, many *ulama* argued that the authoritative instructions regarding the *hudud* punishments contained so many conditions that they were hardly ever applied. For instance, adultery is punishable by death if confirmed by four witnesses, each of whom knows that giving false witness on illicit sexual conduct is itself a crime deserving the death penalty. Jurists used this argument to limit the application of these punishments as much as possible, but there was no agreement among them. Today, in some Muslim countries, the government has reintroduced the *hudud* punishments to convince the people that it resists the cultural pressure of the West and that its rule is faithful to the Quran, while in fact its rule leaves people in poverty and refuses to educate them, thereby disregarding the Quran.

Tariq Ramadan finds the physical punishments practised in these Muslim countries objectionable. Yet since these punishments are decreed in the sacred texts, he knows that it will not be easy to abolish them. According to the Islamic tradition, it would be possible to invalidate them if the *ulama* in Muslim countries arrived at an agreement, taking into account the intention of *sharia*, that these punishments should be modified according to contemporary sensibilities. Only the consensus of the *ulama* could effect this change. In March 2005, Ramadan proposed a moratorium on these punishments: he asked the governments of Muslim countries to stop applying the *hudud* so as allow the *ulama* in all parts to re-examine this issue in perfect freedom. Many critics in France were scandalized by Ramadan's call for a moratorium: according to them, the right thing for him to do would have been to condemn these punishments unconditionally. Yet Ramadan wanted to do more than condemn them; he hoped that a consensus of the *ulama* would abolish them.

Reading Ramadan's critics convinced me that they had not read the long statement in which this theologian had proposed the moratorium, even though it was and continues to be available on the Internet.[83] His statement is a passionate effort to mobilize all Muslim men and women, especially those living in Muslim countries, so that they do the following:

i) urge the governments of Muslim countries to stop applying the corporal punishments to make room for a free debate among the *umala*,

ii) persuade the *ulama* to have the courage to denounce the instrumentalization of Islam to humiliate women and men,

iii) foster the education of the masses, teaching them that
a literalist conformity to a Quranic text does not assure
fidelity to Islam,

iv) convince them that listening to ethical values of outsiders is not a surrender to the Western powers, and

v) teach them that what makes a society faithful to Islam
is not the application of repressive measures and cruel
punishments, but the political will to promote social
and economic justice and protect the integrity of every
individual, woman and man. If the *umala* come to an
agreement, the *hudud* punishments will be abolished.

A reading of Ramadan's statement reveals that its author
repudiated these punishments and supports a movement in
the worldwide Muslim community for their abolishment.

*

In this chapter we have seen that *sharia* guides believers
in the Muslim way of life. It is not a legal code; it consists,
rather, of ethical teaching, ritual instructions, a few concrete
prescriptions plus universal legal principles, the concrete
application of which demands attention to the particular
historical situation. *Sharia* enables Muslims to be faithful to
Islam in various cultures. In the next chapter we shall see
how Ramadan defines fidelity to Islam for Muslims living
in the West.

5

WESTERN MUSLIMS

After explaining the universal message of Islam and the rules for interpreting *sharia*, Ramadan addresses the situation of Muslims in Western societies and offers them pastoral guidance. He begins by describing the difficulties they are likely to encounter.

Who are these Muslims? They are immigrants who came to Europe and North America in recent decades and who now have children and grandchildren born in their new society. Their entry into the secular democratic culture of the West offered them political freedom and the protection of the law, which they greatly appreciated. At the same time, this culture fosters values through schools, mass media and commercial advertising that are at odds with the Islamic way of life. Muslims react to this situation in a variety of ways. Some of them take advantage of the new circumstances, join the competitive race and become upwardly mobile. In doing so, they bracket their Muslim identity. Others choose to remain faithful to their cultural tradition and willingly live as strangers in their new society. Ramadan observes that

Muslims keen on protecting their inherited identity often emphasize the visible signs of their religion, especially the dress code, more than they did when they lived in their country of origin. It would be unfortunate, Ramadan writes, if Muslims come to regard the external practices as the essence of their faith, forgetting the primary summons to worship God, live humbly and do good to one's fellow human beings. Arguing that the future of Muslims in the West is neither assimilation nor self-isolation, Ramadan is glad that a growing number of Muslims have become active citizens of their society, practising their faith and making a contribution to the common good. He observes that the second and third generations of these Muslims are no longer familiar with the culture of their ancestors: they have become Westerners.

Another source of the difficulties Muslims experience in Western societies is the wave of prejudice they encounter – prejudice against foreigners, against people of non-European origin, against exotic religions, against Islam. Over the last decade, and not only as a result of September 11, 2001, the wave of prejudice has become stronger in Western societies. In many countries there are now political parties hostile to immigrants. These parties try to persuade people that the presence of foreigners threatens the nation's cultural identity. Ramadan reports that many Westerners have the idea that Islam is a religion that demands cultural uniformity, promotes hostility to Western civilization and refuses to honour personal freedom and human rights. The best-known scholarly expression of this opinion is Samuel Huntington's theory of the clash of civilizations.[84]

Ramadan has given many lectures, written many articles and published many books to defend Islam against the objections constantly raised against it. Yet in his two major books, in which he addresses Muslims in the West – *To Be a European Muslim* and *Western Muslims and the Future of Islam* – his concern is quite different: it is properly theological. In these two books he explores what fidelity to Islam means for Western Muslims. What does the God in whom they believe expect of them? What does *sharia* demand of them, living as they do in Western societies?

The new context

It will not surprise the reader that Ramadan refuses to answer this question without first examining what the Islamic schools of law say about Muslims living in non-Muslim countries. Only after showing that their teaching no longer addresses the contemporary reality does he make his own proposal.

These schools of law made a clear distinction between Muslim and non-Muslim lands: the Muslims regions were called *dar al-Islam* (abode of Islam) and the hostile regions *dar al-harb* (abode of war). The *ulama* of the different schools did not agree on the definition of these terms. For some of them, *dar al-Islam* referred to a land where the population was Muslim. For others, it referred to countries ruled by Islamic law. For still others, it designated places where Muslims were safe and protected. *Dar al-harb* referred to re-

gions where Muslims stood alone, were exposed to dangers
and unprotected by law. According to these schools of law,
Muslims could be visitors in these regions, but they could
not settle there. Today, some Muslims brought up on this
ancient teaching ask themselves the anguishing question
whether integrating into a Western society is permitted
by God. The *Salafi* literalists, Ramadan notes, still defend
the distinction between *dar al-Islam* and *dar al-harb*: they
look upon the West as a hostile region and demand that
their followers living in the West isolate themselves from
mainstream society.

Many *ulama* recognize that referring to the non-Muslim
world as *dar al-harb* (abode of war) has become unrealistic.
Some have proposed to call it *dar al-ahad* (abode of treaty),
since international law and intergovernmental agreements
assure the safety of Muslims in non-Muslim lands. Ramadan
makes a more radical analysis of the present situation. He
argues that the neat division of the world into two distinct
spheres no longer makes sense. The so-called Muslim countries are no longer societies ruled by Islamic law. Under the
impact of colonization and, subsequently, as willing participants in the capitalist economic system, these societies
have adopted many laws based on Western models. Their
governments often violate Islamic teaching by refusing to
foster the education of the people, turning a deaf ear to their
voices and suppressing their movements of reform. At the
same time, the non-Muslim world has also undergone great
changes. Millions of Muslims now live in Europe and the
Americas as loyal citizens, not simply as temporary guests.

Because of the widening gap between the wealthy countries of the West and the poorer countries of rest of the world, massive immigration to Western societies will continue, and Muslims will become ever more numerous in them. In the present historical situation, the twofold division of the world offered by traditional Islamic jurisdiction no longer applies.

Because neither the Quran nor the Sunna mention the twofold division of the world, Ramadan feels free to propose his own theological interpretation of the present context. As a *Salafi* reformer, his first step is to reread the Quran for inspiration. He notices that when residing in Mecca at the beginning of his ministry, the Prophet and his followers lived in a pluralistic society where some people were friendly and others hostile. The Prophet called upon believers to give witness (*shahada*) to their faith and manifest it by their good works. To give witness, Ramadan argues, is the primary religious duty of Muslims today, living as they do in a pluralistic situation. Whether they live in the West or in countries where the majority is Muslim, their situation is theologically speaking *dar al-shahada*, the place where they must give witness of their faith.[85] The world is not divided into two spheres, Ramadan argues. The doctrine of the One God, *tahwid*, prompts him to say that the world is one: one in its origin and one in its destiny. He recalls the words of the Prophet: "The whole world is my mosque."[86]

This theology of place, Ramadan argues, delivers Muslims in the West from the question of whether their presence in the West is permitted only as a passing phase, or whether their integration into a Western society is truly God's will. Ramadan refers here to the rule of permissibility (discussed in the previous chapter) that encourages Muslims to open themselves to the entire created order, to new cultures and distant lands, with very few prohibitions.

Moving further in his inquiry, Ramadan asks whether Muslims living in the West are by this very fact frustrated in their essential being. Should they be dreaming of living elsewhere, or can they fulfill their vocation as committed believers in the West? To reply to this question, Ramadan develops the idea that the blossoming of the Muslim personality requires five areas of freedom. Here is a brief summary of his idea:

i) Because Muslims believe in the One God and have a spiritual life, they want to live in a society where their religious commitment is respected.

ii) Because Muslims worship their God in community, they want to live a society that protects their religious liberty.

iii) To live in security Muslims need more than mere tolerance; they want their rights to be protected by law.

iv) Because Muslims are held to give testimony to Islam, they want the freedom to announce and explain their faith in public.

v) Because Muslims are urged by their faith to act in social affairs and foster social justice, they want to live in a society where they are able to participate in the political life.[87]

Ramadan continues his argument by demonstrating that these five areas of freedom are guaranteed in Western democratic societies. Despite certain limitations imposed on Muslims in regard to particular practices, and despite the prejudice to which Muslims are often exposed, the law of their society protects their freedom: their faith is respected, they have religious liberty, their rights are guaranteed, they enjoy freedom of expression, and they can participate in political life. Ramadan concludes that Muslims living in Western society are not prevented by this fact from fulfilling their religious vocation. There is no need for them to dream of living elsewhere: they are able to thrive as Muslims where they are.

Responsible citizenship

Ramadan continues his inquiry into the situation of Muslims in Western society, in light of their faith. He offers a theological argument to demonstrate that *sharia* demands of Muslim obedience to the laws of the country in which they live, except when a particular law violates Muslim moral principles. Contracts, Ramadan argues, are taken very seriously in Islam.[88] The Prophet insisted that persons or groups who have made a contract with a partner must remain faithful to it – under all circumstances, even if this should be gravely inconvenient. The Prophet himself acted upon this belief in his life. Once he was established in Medina, the Prophet made a pact with the hostile tribes of Quraysh in Mecca, agreeing that if someone were to leave Medina for Mecca, he would be allowed to stay there, but if someone were to escape from Mecca, the Prophet would not accept him but send him back to Mecca. Later, when a man who had converted to Islam escaped from Mecca, the Prophet, faithful to the contract, refused to receive him – a decision that amazed his companions. Contracts are binding, even when they demand a sacrifice.

Ramadan continues his argument by claiming that a Muslim who applies for an entry visa into a country, accepts employment in it, or becomes a naturalized citizen is implicitly committing himself or herself to a contract, promising to follow the laws of that country. Since contracts are binding under all circumstances, *sharia* obliges Muslims to obey the laws of their country, unless a particular law violates Islamic teaching, in which case they can invoke the freedom of conscience position – just as other citizens do when a law violates their deep moral convictions. This argument, based on fidelity to contracts, confirms the argument mentioned in chapter 3 based on the rule that when the Quran gives no clear instruction, Muslims are to act in a way that serves the common good.

Some Muslims may still worry whether living in non-Muslim societies and associating with non-Muslim men and women is fully acceptable from the point of view of their faith. Ramadan thinks that this worry demands careful attention. What is needed, he says, is to go back to the Islamic sources, the Quran and the Sunna. There we find many texts that approve of Muslims living and associating with non-Muslims. The Prophet attached great importance to the biblical story of Joseph, a believer in the One God, who lived in Egypt among non-believers and even accepted a high position in the government. The Prophet himself lived in Mecca among non-believers, some of whom were his friends, especially his uncle Abu Talib, who never abandoned his old Arab beliefs. When Muslims suffered persecution in Mecca, the Prophet received God's permission to send some members of the community to safety. They went to Abyssinia where an-Najashi, the Christian Negus, welcomed them, and where they lived among non-Muslims who respected them.[89] Later, when the persecution in Mecca intensified, the Prophet and his companion Abu Bakr decided to save themselves by secretly leaving the city and travelling to Medina. They were guided on this dangerous journey by Ibn Urayqat, a friend and trustworthy polytheist. Ramadan cites other examples of cooperation between the Prophet and non-believers on the basis of trust and competence. These experiences, Ramadan argues, reveal the fundamental principle guiding relations between Muslims and non-Muslims: respect and the willingness to work together doing good.

Faithful Muslims should become good citizens in Western societies. Again and again Ramadan tells Western Muslims to stop thinking of themselves as a minority and instead recognize themselves as citizens. While they may at times be obliged to defend their rights as members of a minority suffering discrimination, they must not forget that as citizens they are to make their contribution to the common good and be co-responsible for justice and peace in society. Ramadan notes that political parties sometimes choose candidates with an Arab name to attract the votes of Muslims. Warning Muslims not to give in to such misguided loyalties, Ramadan repeats that Muslims are committed first of all to justice and the other universal virtues. They will want to vote for the party whose program furthers social justice and the well-being of all citizens. We shall return to Ramadan's understanding of social justice further on.

There can be no doubt that Ramadan advocates the integration of Muslims into the Western society to which they belong. At the same time he is strongly opposed to assimilation. He recognizes that the dominant culture in the West puts enormous pressures on Muslims, especially the secular assumptions that underlie public life. Here religion is honoured if it remains purely private. More than that, Islam seems to frighten many Westerners: not only does it represent a new religious presence in their midst, it is also seen as seen promoting hostility to Western culture. Exposed to this cultural pressure, many Muslims drift into assimilation, disappear in the crowd and cease to bear witness to the One God. The percentage of Muslims who become unbelievers is considerable.

One reaction against this loss of the Muslim identity is the turn of many young Muslims to the Islam of the Prophet and his Companions, imitating as much as possible their way of life and the clothes they wore. The desire to rescue the Muslim identity explains the success of the *Salafi* literalists in Europe. We have noted several times that Ramadan regards the literalists' interpretation of Islam as inauthentic: it overlooks the universal message of Islam, and it ignores the abiding relevance of Islam in the changing conditions of history. For him, the literalists produce a false image of Islam.

Another reaction to the secularizing pressure of Western society is the tendency among many Muslims to form ethnic communities, such as Algerian or Pakistani, preserve their local customs, and educate their children in the culture they have brought with them. Yet what they hand on to their children, Ramadan observes, is a North African or Asian Islam, an Islam that does not address the experience of living in the West and for that reason is not likely to survive for very long. Ramadan regrets that Muslims in their new society tend to organize themselves on an ethnic basis and fail to realize that they belong to the *umma*, the community of the faithful, blessed by God. Too often, the stress on ethnicity keeps their organizations and even their mosques isolated from one another. For the future flourishing of Islam in the West, Ramadan concludes, solidarity among Muslims and the joint confession of their faith are of utmost importance.

Ramadan rejects both assimilation and isolation. What he advocates is the integration of Muslims into modern society in a manner that protects and enhances their identity as believers. Ramadan looks with admiration to the presence of Jews in modern society, fully integrated and at the same time proudly celebrating their Jewish identity. Should this not also be possible for Muslims? Muslims, he writes, must come to understand who they are and what they stand for. They must define their identity themselves, not take it from the society that misjudges them nor from Muslims who refuse to face up to modernity. "It is only by acting in this way that European Muslims will feel that they are subjects of their own history, accountable before God, responsible before mankind. To be subjects of their own history also means that they will eventually go beyond the pernicious feeling of being foreigners, of being different, of being an obvious manifestation of an insoluble problem."[90]

Collective identity

Ramadan defines the identity of Western Muslims in religious terms without reference to the cultural elements brought by the immigrants from Africa or Asia. In response to the present situation, Western Muslims should define their identity by four engagements involving their faith:[91]

i) The spiritual dimension: testifying to the One God, practising the pillars of Islam, enjoying membership in the *umma* and exploring the spiritual life.

ii) The intellectual dimension: studying the Islamic tradition, recognizing its contemporary relevance and being ready to keep on learning.

iii) The communicative dimension: handing on the faith to the next generation and explaining the faith to the wider society.

iv) The practical dimension: promoting justice in society and serving the common good in other ways.

Leaving behind their cultural inheritance as Africans or Asians does not mean that Western Muslims strive for assimilation. Their faith in Islam makes them welcome the elements of modern society that enhance human life and warns them against elements that estrange men and women from their human vocation. As Muslims, they will be critical citizens, participating in public debates and resisting the dominant individualism, utilitarianism and secularism. Their faith urges them to be in solidarity with their society and at the same time judge its unjust practices and alienating culture. Rooted in Islam, they have a message for society: they promote the universal virtues and proclaim their faith in God. Their integration into society is dialogical: they listen, welcome the truth they hear, stand against error and bring new light.

This is, in fact, how Jews and Christians who take their faith seriously react to modern, secular society. Their integration is dialogical: they are in critical conversation with the society with which they are in solidarity.

To achieve a secure common identity, Western Muslims will have to arrive at a consensus regarding the interpretation of *sharia*. Ramadan suggests that Muslims living in the West should cease to listen to the *umala* from the East, living as they do in different historical contexts. Western Muslims will have to rely on *ulama* who live in the West. Since the *fatwa* pronounced by individual Western *ulama* are not always unanimous, what is needed in the West are councils or associations where *ulama* work together, arrive at agreements and provide solutions to practical questions that will be widely accepted and promote unity among Muslims. A good beginning is the Fiqh Council (Council

of Islamic Law and Jurisprudence) in the U.S. and the
European Council for Islamic Rulings and Researches
founded in London in 1997.[92]

Subculture or denomination

Reading the writings of Tariq Ramadan with the eye
of a sociologist, I recognize that the Muslim community
he envisages in the West is not "a subculture," but rather
"a denomination." A *subculture* is a collective of people defined by cultural practices that differentiate them from the
majority of the population and assign them to the margin
of society. This is what Muslim communities in the West
often are, but it is not what Ramadan hopes for them. He
wants these communities to be participants in mainstream
society. A *denomination* is a collectivity defined in the sociol-
ogy of religion. European sociologists used to distinguish
between churches and sects, where churches referred to
religious communities that embraced an entire society and
were in dialogue with its dominant culture, while sects
referred to religious minorities that disapproved of the
dominant culture and survived in the margin of society. This
distinction lost its meaning in the United States of America,
because the establishment of a church was excluded by
law. Christians created new institutional forms called "denominations," which, like churches, were in dialogue with
the dominant culture and, like sects, did not embrace the
entire society and represented only a minority.[93] While
there were disagreements among them, the denominations
respected one another and worked together on issues that

served the common good of society. Since the Catholic Church refused to see itself as a denomination and continued to regard Protestants as heretics, Catholics suffered discrimination in America – and thus formed a religious subculture. When the Second Vatican Council (1962–1965) recognized dissident Christians as members of the body of Christ and fostered ecumenical dialogue, the Catholic Church in America became – sociologically speaking – a denomination reconciled to religious pluralism. Jews, Muslims and followers of other religions who came to the U.S. set up organizations that resembled denominations: they respected pluralism and cooperated across denominational lines on civic issues. There have been, and there still are, sects in America that stand apart and live on the margins, but cultural forces operative in society eventually transform them into denominations.

Thanks to the secularization of society and the movements of population, the churches in many European countries have become denominations: they now represent only a minority in society; they are reconciled to religious pluralism; and they address the public not with authority, but with an invitation for dialogue. This is an historical context in which Ramadan urges Muslims to stop acting like a subculture and become a denomination in critical conversation with society as a whole.

In this context I wish to mention a word that has taken on special meaning in France The word *communitarianism* was invented in the 20th century to refer to a political philosophy that criticizes liberal individualism and emphasizes the role of the community in defining and shaping individuals. Communitarians are social liberals. They are not right-wing thinkers who stress community at the expense of personal freedom, nor are they left-wing thinkers who hold that communities do not enjoy shared values since their members are divided by the class conflict. In a French dictionary of ethics and moral philosophy published in 1996, the article on *le communautarisme* still has the same meaning as the corresponding English expression.[94] But more recently, *le communautarisme* has taken on a different meaning in France: it is now defined as a political philosophy that assigns to a religious, ethnic or cultural community a value more important than the universal values of freedom and equality. This shift in the definition of communitarianism in France reveals the anxiety that the presence of Muslim communities have produced in that country. The affirmation of collective religious identities is quickly perceived as a cultural current that undermines republican values and weakens the cohesion of society. In France, Ramadan's pleading for a strong Muslim community is seen by many as the promotion of a dangerous communitarianism. A more careful sociological analysis distinguishing between *subculture* and *denomination* reveals that Ramadan's pastoral message to the Muslim community is to practise the republican virtues in the name of their faith – that is, to become citizens in the full sense, participate in democratic politics and contribute to the common good of society.

Democratic pluralism

We saw in the previous chapter that the Quranic revelation deals with two distinct spheres: the worship of God, and social affairs. The directives for worship are unchanging and applicable everywhere, while the directives for social affairs contain universal principles whose application must take into consideration the concrete historical situation in which the Muslim community finds itself. Living in Western societies obliges Muslim to reread their sacred texts, reflect on the universal principles revealed in them, and discover how they supply guidance for believers in their new society. Ramadan, we saw, finds in the Islamic tradition the imperative for responsible citizenship in democratic societies.

The social involvement of Muslims is an important issue that Ramadan treats at great length. He offers a vigorous refutation of the claims made by *Salafi* literalists and some traditionalists that Muslims must remain strangers and outsiders in Western societies. He summarizes their hasty claims in four main points:

i) There are no "elections" in Islam: for the relation of individuals to their political leader is a contract of allegiance;

ii) Muslims must obey a Muslim ruler, even if he fails to do justice, because a Quranic verse commands Muslims to obey God, the Prophet, and "those who exercise (political) authority";

iii) Since Muslims can give allegiance only to a Muslim, they must abstain from political involvement in the West; and

iv) Muslims may not desire political office since the Prophet said, "we do not give authority to those who ask for it or ardently desire it."[95]

This literalist reading of Islam, Ramadan writes, is promoted by the petromonarchies, especially Saudi Arabia, for their own political purposes. He laments that thanks to their influence, many young people in Europe look upon democracy as *haram* and choose to remain strangers and outsiders in society.

Most traditionalist *ulama* do not follow this literalist interpretation. Recognizing the distinction between *dar al-Islam* and *dar al-harb*, they argue that the rejection of democratic government applies only in *dar al-Islam*, the traditional Muslim countries, and that Muslims living in the Western world, part of *dar al-harb*, are dispensed from this Islamic rule and may participate in democratic life. Why are they dispensed? Because necessity obliges them, and necessity allows Muslims to be dispensed from general regulations.[96]

Ramadan offers a vigorous refutation of this legal argument. He argues, on the contrary, that the condition of Muslims in Western society calls for a rethinking of the ethic of governance in all parts of the world, including Muslim countries.

His reasoning reminds the Catholic reader of a parallel argument in Catholic theology. In the nineteenth century, as we saw in chapter 1, the papacy repeatedly condemned human rights, especially religious liberty, a measure that embarrassed Catholics who were minorities in their country of residence. These Catholics were in need of religious liberty. To take their situation into consideration, the Church's official teaching proposed that only in countries where Catholics were the majority did they have to insist that the government protect the true faith and deny religious liberty. In countries where Catholics were a minority, they were allowed to defend religious liberty. We noted in chapter 1 that Maritain eventually rejected this kind of opportunistic reasoning. He argued that the experience of Catholics living in modern democracies called for a rethinking of the ethic of governance in the entire Catholic world, including the so-called Catholic countries. He therefore supported the movement within the Catholic Church for the recognition of human rights.

Ramadan, as we saw above, rejects the division of the world in *dar al-Islam* and *dar al-harb* and offers a theological interpretation of the present historical context as the *dar al-shahada*, the abode of witness. Muslims in all parts, including those living in traditional Muslim countries, are now bound to return to Islamic sources, clarify the universal principles revealed in them, and then inquire how they are to be applied in the present historical situation. The Islamic legal tradition had always recognized that when a social issue emerges on which the sources are silent, the *ulama* must use interpretation (*ijtihad*), deriving new meaning from the sacred texts by following a set of rules. In the last chapter, I mentioned three rules to which Ramadan pays special attention: i) recognizing Islam's "permissibility" or openness to the new, ii) taking into account the intension of *sharia*, and iii) promoting the common good of society. If I read him correctly, Ramadan applies these rules of interpretation in his treatment of the Islamic teaching on democracy and responsible citizenship.

There are good reasons why Ramadan offers an extended argument to refute the idea that Muslims fuse the two orders of religion and politics and expect society to be ruled by divinely given laws, the *sharia*. Many people in the West think that the Muslim tradition has no equivalent for the separation of Church and state. The radical Muslims whom Ramadan designates as political literalists actually make the claim that Islam calls for an Islamic state. In line with other reformist thinkers, Ramadan rejects this idea, even for countries with a majority Muslim population. He offers two reasons for his position. First, a just society must be built up from below. Islam demands that Muslims be virtuous, practise justice and compassion, look after their families and jointly build a peace-loving society, yet virtuous living cannot be imposed from above. Virtuous living is nourished from below by the spiritual life of faith and daily Islamic practice. Such a way of living presupposes people's freedom – the freedom to surrender themselves to God wholeheartedly. Second, a just society needs critical citizens. Since Ramadan interprets the world as the abode of witness (*dar al-shahada*), he recognizes in Muslim faith a critical or prophetic dimension that judges the existing order in the light of God's revelation. Since an Islamic state does not permit the critical debate among citizens, it does not provide the freedom that Muslims need to give witness to their faith.

Ramadan admits, of course, that in the history of Islam, societies were usually governed by Muslim rulers who protected and promoted Islam, very much like Western societies ruled by Christian kings who protected and promoted the Church in their realm. After the Peace of Westphalia in 1648, the religion of the prince even determined the religion of his people: *cuius regio, eius religio*. This meant that there was no place for religious liberty. The separation of Church and state has been a modern development. Ramadan repeatedly tells his audience in France that as a Muslim *ulama*, he welcomes the French law of 1905 that created the radical separation of Church and state.[97] He argues that Muslims should be grateful for the neutrality of the modern state in regard to religion: this is a condition for their flourishing. But even in majority Muslim societies, Ramadan holds, the state should guarantee the freedom of religion as well as the freedom of expression that is the precondition for critical public debates.

At the same time, Ramadan strongly defends the traditional teaching that faith in Islam calls for an active engagement in society. He interprets the four pillars of Islam as a summons to social solidarity:

i) The ritual prayer performed several times a day creates a community of heart and soul among the faithful;

ii) alms-giving is a contribution to a more just distribution of goods – in fact, Ramadan suggests that in modern so-

ciety, these alms should no longer be given to the poor
of one's choice, but be administered as a tax contribution
and directed to the people most in need;

iii) the ritual fasting makes believers participate in the hun-
ger suffered by the poor all over the world; and

iv) the pilgrimage to Mecca offers a religious experience
that delivers Muslims from a narrow identification with
their tribe, ethnicity or nation and reveals to them the
boundary-transcending solidarity of their faith.

Islam is a society-building faith. The Quranic revelation
includes directives for setting up a just and peaceful society
that believers are to implement. Surrender to God implies
faith and works, where works include making society just
and pleasing to God. For Muslims living in Western democracies, this means participation in social and political life
in the name of their faith, both to defend their rights and
to promote the common good of society.

I have the impression that it is this message that makes
Ramadan a controversial figure in France. There, if I understand the situation correctly, religious faith is respected
as the spiritual journey chosen by individual citizens, yet
it is not tolerated as the public creed motivating political
engagement in society. Catholics also have a social teaching
that prompts them – or should prompt them – to become
actors in public life. As I explained in chapter 1, in the past
Catholic social teaching was based simply on natural law
theory, but since the pontificate of John XXIII, Catholic
social teaching is an expression of the truth revealed in the

Gospel. Catholics in France, having accepted *la laïcité* or the secularization of the state, have learned to be modest and not to articulate the faith implicit in their public engagements. In fact, Cardinal Lustiger, the late Archbishop of Paris, once asked the Muslims of France to learn to live with *la laïcité*, just as Catholics have had to do.

In Britain and Canada, social engagement in the name of religion is fully accepted. For example, the Cooperative Commonwealth Federation (CCF), the social-democratic party of Canada, was founded in 1933 by a political movement inspired in part by the Protestant Social Gospel. The New Democratic Party (NDP), the successor of the CCF, adopted an increasingly secular tone and avoided a religious vocabulary. At the national NDP convention in 2006, several Members of Parliament, regretting the party's purely secular discourse, called a meeting of all the party members who were socialists for religious reasons: 300 arrived, including some Jews and Muslims. By contrast, in Quebec, at one time a uniformly Catholic society, Catholic social activists do not advertise their religious conviction.

As mentioned earlier, Ramadan tells Western Muslims not to think of themselves as minorities, but rather as citizens ready to work with other citizens to create a more just society. Seeing oneself as belonging to a minority is a psychologically debilitating experience capable of producing an inferiority complex or a self-perception of being a victim and thus unable to act freely. Summoned by their God, Muslims want to defend their rights in society and, more important, promote with other citizens social and political policies that embody the universal values of solidarity, equality and justice. Ramadan provides a substantial introduction to a Muslim social and economic ethics.[98]

The Catholic reader is surprised by the similarity between this Muslim social ethics and the recent social teaching of the Catholic Church. These teachings, offered in the name of the respective faith, include the dignity of the human person, support for human rights, the freedom to participate in political life, and the commitment to solidarity, beginning with the poor and excluded.

Both Muslim and Catholic teaching denounce the unregulated market economy that respects no ethical principles. For many centuries, the Catholic Church condemned as gravely sinful the taking of interest for money loaned. Interest taking was seen as exploitative: it was called usury. Calvin was the first Christian theologian who recognized the changed role of money in society and defended the legitimacy of earning interest on capital loaned. Subsequently, the Catholic Church also became reconciled to a capitalist economy as long as it was restrained by ethical principles. According to the present Catholic *Catechism*, "regulating the economy solely by the law of the marketplace fails social justice."[99] More drastic is this statement of Pope Paul VI: "Unchecked liberalism leads to dictatorship producing the international imperialism of money."[100] The Muslim tradition condemned and continues to condemn the taking of interest on money loaned. Ramadan admits that, in actual fact, not only Western Muslims and but also Muslim countries that claim to be guardians of orthodox Islam participate in the capitalist world economy. Even Islamic banks that offer their clients an alternative to interest on their savings are in some way linked to and dependent on the world economy. What is needed, according to Ramadan, is an alternative economic system, one that is non-exploitative and geared toward a more just distribution of wealth. Is it possible, he asks himself, to resist the present unregulated market economy? Here is his reply:

> It seems to me that a new alternative based in the West must be put forward ... It is absolutely vital that Muslims study closely and deeply the dynamics of resistance [against the neo-liberal economy] that are already in process in America and Europe. Muslims are neither the first nor the only ones to reject the dominant economic system: many studies have been published and development cooperatives, alternative banks, and ethical businesses and investment funds are functioning, putting forward [an alternative practice]. Muslim citizens should take inspiration from these writings and experiences and get involved in multidimensional, complementary and long-term partnerships.[101]

We saw in chapter 1 that with Paul VI's 1967 encyclical *Populorum progressio*, the Church's official teaching communicated to Catholics "a third-world consciousness" – the troubling awareness of the scandalous division of humanity into 20 per cent of the population that consumed 80 per cent of the earth's natural resources and 80 per cent of the population that relied on 20 per cent of these same resources. This was an injustice, Paul VI wrote, that "cries to heaven."[102] Looking at the distribution of wealth and power in the world from a Muslim perspective persuades Ramadan to communicate "a third-world consciousness" to Western

Muslims.[103] They cannot have a realistic understanding of their own situation in the North without the disconcerting awareness of the misery spreading in most countries of the South. Some journalists in France found Ramadan's *tiers-mondisme* opportunistic and unrelated to his true concerns.[104] Yet his solidarity with humanity's disadvantaged majority is perfectly in keeping with his theology of *tahwid*, the One God drawing into oneness humanity fragmented by disobedience.

Men and women

Ramadan's theology of citizenship also applies to women. With embarrassment and sorrow he recognizes that women suffer humiliating subjugation in Muslim societies, and are subject to discrimination even in Muslim communities established in the West. In many Western Muslim families, the wife is subservient to her husband; sons are given education and freedom, while the lives of daughters are strictly controlled. Ramadan laments that even in the West, the presence of women is not always welcome at mosques and other Muslim organizations. He finds this situation scandalous. In his book *Western Muslims and the Future of Islam*, the title for the chapter on women is "The birth of an Islamic feminism."[105]

With Muslim feminists, Ramadan argues that the subjugation of women in Muslim societies is a cultural inheritance legitimated by a few texts of the Quran and the Sunna, while the universal teaching of Islam recognizes the equality of men and women before God, the complementary role of men and woman in the family, and the rights of women to education and economic independence. Islamic feminists also remember the strong women in company of the Prophet, especially his first wife, Khadija, an independent businesswoman, and his later wife, Aisha, who exercised leadership in the community at certain moments. Ramadan recognizes that in the past, women tended to be looked upon as mothers, wives or daughters. What is new today, he argues, is that Muslim women are beginning to see themselves as women – not simply defined by their social role, but as persons, as responsible agents. What is also new, he writes, is that women have become Islamic scholars who do their own research, their own reading of the sacred texts, and their own theology. This independent thinking and acting, Ramadan admits, challenges the cultural inheritance of the Muslim community, even in Western countries. He insists all the same that Islamic feminism is not a concession to the West: it started as a theological current produced at the end of the nineteenth century by intellectual Muslim women in Egypt who were associated with *al-nadah*, the Islamic renewal movement.[106]

Islamic feminists acknowledge that men and women play complementary roles in the family and society, yet they want to define themselves what this complementarity means. Nobody denies the complementarity of men and women in the procreation of human beings: men become fathers, and women, mothers. But what is the cultural meaning of complementarity? Does it mean that the role of men is to make decisions and give orders, and the role of women is to obey? Does complementarity mean that women may not exercise leadership in society? Does the right ordering of their relationship mean that the husband is the bread-winner and the wife looks after the house and the children? Ramadan argues that men and women together will have to define what complementarity means for them.

Living in the material conditions of the West has a strong cultural impact on the Muslim family. Financial obligations often demand that both husband and wife work outside the home. Since middle-class people no longer have maids, the question arises whether husbands and sons should help the mother in the kitchen and in cleaning the house. Life in contemporary society inevitably leads to the rethinking of the roles of men and women. A recent article in the popular magazine *The American Muslim* showed that the Prophet helped with the dishes in the kitchen, and that therefore husbands coming home from work should not think that their faith dispenses them from helping their wives with domestic tasks.[107]

Should Muslim women be veiled? The Quran calls for modesty in dress for men and women. Wearing the veil is not a big issue in itself: in some Muslim communities, women are veiled, and in others they are not. Yet for various reasons, the veil has recently become a big issue in France and other Western countries. Many Muslim women have decided to wear the veil as a sign of their faith, their identity and their resistance to Western assimilation. Other Muslim women have reluctantly started to put on the veil because of pressure to do so by forces within their community. Meanwhile, some Muslims in the West have denounced the veil as a symbol of women's subordination. In some countries, women may not wear the veil at schools and universities. Ramadan strongly defends the freedom of women. He demands that they not be pressured by the Muslim community nor by the government, but be allowed to make up their mind whether they wish to wear the veil.

Ramadan has been criticized because he defends the freedom of women in Islam in a general way without clearly saying that he rejects certain Islamic practices, such as polygamy and the husband's unilateral right to repudiate his wife. I have heard this criticism from members of the Canadian Council of Muslim Women. The well-known Muslim jurist Mohamed Charfi also complained that Ramadan remains too vague in his defence of women's rights. "It is not sufficient to say that Islam is a religion that is good and just and loves women without making a clear statement on key issues. A Muslim thinker must openly declare his opposition to polygamy and the right of repudiation so that we know where he stands."[108]

It is my impression that Ramadan does not state his opposition to polygamy and the right of repudiation because these practices are illegal in the West and thus forbidden for Western Muslims. At the same time, he is blunt and outspoken in his criticism of Western Muslims because of their attachment to cultural practices that subjugate women.

> Some in Europe and the United States do not allow women to enter mosques, and if, by happy chance, there is a place for them, it is usually dilapidated and often even without

a good sound system. Imams find "Islamic" justifications for "fast-track" marriages, without any preparatory official administrative procedures, leaving women without security or rights, abused and deceived by unscrupulous individuals. Divorce is made very difficult, even when it is clear that the women are defending their most basic rights. Some women, with the knowledge of all around her, suffer violence and degradation, while the Muslim community remains culpable, silent and complicit ... One also finds all sorts of restrictions to do with women, such as the "Islamic" prohibition against their working, having social involvements, speaking in public, and engaging in politics. And what have we not heard about the impossibility of "mixing"! It is true that these practices have sometimes been affirmed and advised in the countries of emigration, and one can certainly find *ulama* in the traditionalist and literalist schools who declare that these are Islamic teachings. But it is essential that we go back to the scriptural sources to evaluate these practices and draw a clear distinction between customs that are culturally based and Islamic principles.[109]

Ramadan, I conclude, is an ally of Islamic feminism.

Religious pluralism

In defining their attitude toward religious pluralism, Muslim and Christian theologians find themselves in similar situations. Christians find in their Scriptures harsh sayings that leave no space for other religions, and generous verses that express God's care for the entire world. To which texts shall Christians assign priority? In Mark's Gospel we read, "Whoever believes and is baptized will be saved, and whoever does not believe will be condemned" (Mk 16:16). Many other verses in the New Testament provide arguments for the subsequent ecclesiastical teaching that "outside the

Church there is no salvation." In the fifteenth century, the Council of Florence declared that pagans, Jews, heretics and schismatics go to hell immediately after they die.[110] It was only at the Second Vatican Council (1962–1965) that the Catholic Church changed its mind and recognized, in reliance on John 1:9, that God's Word resounded in the whole of history and thus also in the world religions.[111] Thanks to this conciliar teaching, the Church now recommends interreligious dialogue and cooperation in the service of the common good.

The Quran contains passages that offer a positive interpretation of religious pluralism for which there are no equivalents in the Bible. According to these passages, religious pluralism has been decreed by God for the benefit of humankind. Ramadan quotes them.[112] "Had God so willed, He would have united them [human beings] in guidance, so do not be among the ignorant" (Quran 6:35). "If your Lord had so willed, everyone on earth would have believed. Is it for you to compel people to believe?" (Quran 10:99). "O people, we have created you from a male and a female, we have divided you into nations and tribes so that you might know one another" (Quran 49:13). "If God had willed, he would have made you one community, but things are as they are to test you in what He has given you. So compete with each other in doing good" (Quran 5:48). These passages suggest that religious pluralism is God's will and that people belonging to different traditions should get to know one another and compete in doing good. This positive evaluation of religious pluralism is in keeping with the universal teaching of Islam (which we studied in chapter 2), according to which God's breath remains with the human beings created by Him, imprinting on their hearts the *fitra* that orients them toward the life of virtue and allows them to discover their need of God.

Ramadan also deals with the harsh sayings of the Quran. There are verses that define Jews and Christians, even though they are among "the people of the book," as *kuffar* (plural of *kafir*), usually translated as infidels or miscreants. "They are certainly in a state of denial (*kafara*), those who have said that God was the messiah, the son of Mary" (Quran 5:17) or "Those among the people of the book and the polytheists who have denied (*kafaru*)" (Quran 98:1). Literalist scholars argue that these sayings reveal the fate of non-Muslims, especially since the Quran adds that "religion in the sight of God is Islam" (Quran 3:19) and "those who desire religion other than Islam will not find themselves accepted and in the hereafter will be among the losers" (Quran 3:85). There are Quranic passages that urge believers to distrust Jews and Christians and refuse cooperation with them, unless in cases of emergency.

Ramadan rejects the interpretation of the literalists because it is in disagreement with Islam's universal teaching. That religion in the sight of God is Islam suggests to him that surrender to God wherever it takes place, in whatever religion, is simply Islam. For many Islamic thinkers even the flowers, the birds and the mountains are Muslims because they worship God in their being. Putting the Quranic verses that warn against infidels and miscreants in their historical context, Ramadan argues, allows one to recognize that they were uttered at occasions when the believing community was seriously challenged and Muslims were tempted to return to the religious traditions from which they had come. The harsh Quranic verses cited above may not be used to invalidate the more open teaching that religious pluralism is due to God's gracious design.

Progressive Catholic theologians deal with the harsh passages of the Bible by giving priority to the universal Christian teaching: that is, humanity created and redeemed by God. They limit the meaning of the harsh passages to the context in which they were uttered. Yet they also apply a hermeneutical principle that Ramadan does not invoke: they read Scripture while taking seriously "the signs of the times." In a world deeply divided between rich and poor regions, threatened by cultural and religious conflicts and wounded by wars and other forms of violence, believers turn to the Bible to hear God's Word of rescue from the present disaster. They refuse to cite biblical texts that appear to legitimate hostility and non-cooperation. It is the disruptive global disunity, the ominous sign of the times, that has urged the Church to rethink its mission in the world and interpret it as witnessing its faith in Jesus Christ by promoting peace and justice and helping to mend a broken world.

Ramadan does not invoke this hermeneutical principle, yet it is operative in his thinking in an implicit way. He, too, feels that Muslims have to rethink the meaning of *dawa*, the call to conversion addressed to outsiders. The reformist thinker Asghar Engineer wrote a report of a meeting attended by the religious leaders of Macedonia, the only republic created after the collapse of Yugoslavia in which there had been no violent conflict. The religious leaders – Orthodox Christians, Muslims, Jews and Protestants – discussed among themselves what they should do to preserve the peace. A Muslim speaker recognized that Christians have the mission to convert the world and Muslims have their *dawa*, but if they do this here in Macedonia, they will provoke massive violence. Our choice, he said, is between dialogue or death.[113] Macedonia may well be the symbol of today's global society.

Addressing himself to Western Muslims who live in a context where it is easy to associate with people of other faiths, Ramadan recommends to them interreligious dialogue, which, he argues, is a rich educational experience. This is how he describes the spiritually beneficial effects of dialogue among believers belonging to different religions:

i)   Recognition of the legitimacy of each other's conviction and respect for them;
ii)   Listening to what people say about their own spiritual sources and not what we understand (or want to understand) about them;
iii) The right, in the name of trust and respect, to ask all possible questions, sometimes even the most embarrassing;
iv)   The practice of self-criticism, which consists in knowing how to discern the difference between what the texts say and what our coreligionists make of them, and deciding clearly what is our personal position.[114]

I believe that my presentation of Ramadan's religious thought has remained within the parameters of dialogue as defined by him.

6

RAMADAN CHALLENGED BY LIBERALISM

The renewal movement (*al-nahda*), which Ramadan represents and adapts to the situation of Western Muslims, has been challenged by Muslim theologians whom he calls modernists or liberals. These scholars believe that to make Islam a credible source of faith in the modern world, a more radical break with traditional beliefs is required. Such scholars respect the renewal movement for its effort to make Islam relevant to believers wrestling with the impact of modernity, but argue that this effort has not sufficiently recognized the challenge of contemporary rationality. Ramadan, as we shall see, defends his reformist position against these liberal challenges.

A lively debate among Muslim scholars took place at the conference entitled New Voices in Islam, organized in 2002 by the International Institute for the Study of Islam in the Modern World (ISIM). Well-known Muslim religious thinkers from various parts of the world were invited to participate.[115] A summary of the presentations and an analysis of the subsequent debates were produced by Michel Hoebink, a member of the International Institute.[116] At the conference, the reformist movement was represented by Tariq Ramadan and the Indian scholar Asghar Engineer, while more liberal forms of Islam were advocated by most of the other participants. It is worth noting the unusual terminology used at the conference: Ramadan and his reformist colleagues were referred to as "modernists."

Engineer presented the case for these "modernists," summarizing the theological approach with which we are familiar from Ramadan's writings. Engineer explained that the Quran contains normative and contextual verses. The normative verses have universal validity, defining mainly the believer's relationship to God; the contextual verses, referring mainly to social relations, must be interpreted by taking into account the concrete historical conditions. The task of the *ulama* is to extract from the contextual verses universal principles that must be applied in various historical circumstances. Traditionalist *ulama* still prescribe the applications worked out between the tenth and twelfth century: having sacralized the past, they refuse to acknowledge the ongoing creativity of Islam. If guided by the universal principles implicit in *sharia*, Islam is capable of addressing all historical situations, including modernity. In an extended argument that resembles Ramadan's theology, Engineer shows that Islam is compatible with human rights and democratic pluralism.

Ramadan added to this argument an idea he has developed in his writings and with which we are now familiar. He proposed that the experience of Muslims in the West

calls for the rethinking of the theological locus of the entire
Muslim community. The traditional distinction between
dar al-Islam and *dar al-harb* no longer describes the present
historical reality. Muslims the world over now live in *dar
al-shahada*, the abode of testimony. Whether they live in the
East or the West, Muslims must give witness to their faith,
profess their ethical vision, denounce the injustices in their
society and thus exercise a prophetic role. It follows from
this point that Ramadan's harsh criticism of the domination
and inequality practised in many Muslim countries is based
not on ideas taken from the West, but on the teaching of
the Quran itself as interpreted in *dar al-shahada*.

For the Catholic reader, the arguments the liberal
Muslim thinkers addressed to the reformist theologians are
interesting, because similar arguments are made by liberal
Christian thinkers against Catholicism and other forms
of classical Christianity. While Islam and Christianity are
quite different religions, the internal debates within the two
communities have a certain similarity.

The liberal objections

From Michel Hoebink's report, entitled *Muslim Intellectuals
and Modern Challenges*, I wish to draw a set of objections raised
by liberal Muslims against the renewal movement.

1. A first objection to the reformist movement was made
by the Tunisian Abdelmajid Charfi, who argued that the
Islam of the Prophet was a divinely revealed ethos, a way
of life and a vision of society that was subsequently misinterpreted by the *ulama*. These jurists interpreted Islam as a

legal system, a set of rules and regulations that had a certain usefulness at the time, but that locked Islam into the social conditions of the past and robbed it of its soul, its ethical vision and creativity. Even though the renewal movement offers a reading of Islam that is relevant to the present age, it still relies on the traditional Islamic schools of law. It is still caught up in the legal thinking of the past.

While Ramadan and Engineer do not deny that legalism is a harmful trend in the practice of Islam, they have great respect for the legal tradition of the early centuries, which revealed the flexibility of Islam and made it speak to many different cultures. They insist, especially for pastoral reasons, that the renewal movement is in harmony with traditional Islam and that ordinary Muslims recognize in the renewal the religion they have inherited. For reformists, the liberal thinkers are professors who speak to the academy, while they, the reformists, address ordinary people and promote a pastoral movement within the Muslim community.

2. According to a second objection, modern rationality demands a critical approach to the Quran. The hermeneutics introduced by the reformist movement is to be praised, but scientific rationality demands a critical examination of the production of the Quran.[117] Since the written text was produced under the early caliphs in response to particular historical circumstances, there is a political dimension in the Quran that deserves attention. Moreover, one can no longer believe that the Prophet remained passive during the divine revelation and simply repeated the words that he heard. Without denying the divine inspiration, modern

thinkers must study the Quran as the work of the Prophet, using principles that apply to all literature. Looking at the Quran as a human book is not incompatible with believing that through this book, God's Word continues to address the Muslim community.

Replying to these proposals, Ramadan says that looking upon the Quran as a human book, and its verses simply as the words of the Prophet, undermines the Muslim faith, based as it is on God's self-revelation in the Quran. The Quran is sacred literature. It may and must be studied with the help of hermeneutic reason, yet as a sacred text it has a transcendent character that cannot be grasped by the critical methods of interpretation applicable to profane literature. Reading the Quran must be done by believers who recognize their need of God. Moreover, theories that question the divine status of the Quran would outrage the Muslim community and have destructive pastoral consequences.

3. The third objection, raised especially by Abdolkarim Soroush and Abdelmajid Charfi, is that the proponents of the reformist movement believe in universal values. The reformists claim that it is possible to extract from the contextual verses of the Quran universal values or principles that can guide the human community in all phases of its history. Yet, according to Soroush and Charfi, universal values are a product of the Western Enlightenment, presuppose worldwide Western domination and have presently been overcome by postmodern thought, the humble recognition of cultural pluralism and the non-universality of values.

Ramadan and Engineer reject the idea that universal values are the production of the Enlightenment. They fear, moreover, that the postmodern discourse of pluralism without shared values encourages dangerous theories, such as the clash of civilizations, that create enemies out of people who are different. Recent interreligious dialogue – for example, at the World Conference of Religions for Peace[118] – has established that the great religious traditions share many core values and that the Golden Rule exists in one form or another in all religious and sapiential traditions. Ramadan recognizes in his writings that universal values are older than the Enlightenment: they are a legacy of the classical Greek tradition, which influenced Late Judaism, Christianity, Islam and, eventually, the Renaissance. I made a brief reference to Islam's encounter with Greek thought in chapter 2. The reformist movement Ramadan represents defends the Universal Declaration of Human Rights and thus – against postmodern fashion – the existence of universal ethical norms.

4. According to a fourth objection, traditional Islam entertains an absolutist understanding of truth that has had devastating historic consequences. Persons and communities in disagreement with Islam are in error, and deserve to be treated as such. The Iranian scholar Abdolkarim Soroush calls for renewed thinking about truth. Truth has many faces; hence, the face to which one is committed is not an absolute. Soroush argues that a certain relativism must be built into the idea of truth so that it does not become a weapon to inflict humiliation upon others.

The Malaysian scholar Farish Noor supported this argument. Islam, he thinks, has an absolutist understanding of
truth that must be overcome. He gave the example of the
Pan-Malaysian Islamic Party (PAS), which followed reformist thinking and respected human rights and religious pluralism as long as it was in a minority position. When it was
elected in the state of Kelantan in 1990, however, the abso-
lutism of Islam took over: the government introduced *sharia*
legislation that reduced political freedom and introduced
the *hubud* penalties, such as capital punishment for apos-
tasy.[119] Progressive Muslims in Malaysia, such as Chandra
Muzzaffar, opposed this development, but they received no
hearing. According to Noor, Islam provides a fundamentally
theocentric discourse based on non-negotiable, universal-
ist and absolute notions of truth, morality, law and order,
contradicting the fundamental democratic principles of free
debate, tolerance and pluralism. As a Muslim believer, Noor
holds that Islam is in need of a more radical transformation
than that introduced by the reformist movement.

Ramadan's reply to this challenge is not recorded in
the report. From his writings, I gather that he thinks the
renewal, *al-nahda*, is sufficient medicine to cure Islam of its
inclination to intolerance and domination. I add to this
point that the Islamic political party in power in Turkey,
sustained by progressive Muslim religious thinkers, honours
democratic pluralism and respects the rights of the religious
minorities.

5. The fifth complaint is that Ramadan's theology and
the renewal movement in general defend the authority of

the *ulama* and refuse to recognize the freedom of all believers to read and interpret the Quran for themselves. We have seen that this is indeed the position defended by Ramadan. The liberal Muslim thinkers demand greater freedom. They recognize that reading the Quran is a spiritual enterprise, yet they hold that the necessary spiritual sensitivity resides in all believers. Believing Muslims are endowed to interpret God's Word addressed to them in the Quran.

Ramadan, as we saw in chapter 4, is afraid that a purely personal reading of the Quran is likely to encourage a literalist interpretation. He realizes, of course, that the literalists, including the political literalists, are able to find *ulama* who bless the fundamentalist reading. I think that the deeper reason why Ramadan rejects free interpretation and defends the authority of the *ulama* is his pastoral endeavour to remain faithful to the great Islamic tradition throughout the ages. He promotes the renewal, he presents himself as a reformist thinker, yet he refuses to overthrow the tradition of the ancients. Ramadan is not a radical. That is why he presents as traditional his innovative hermeneutical principle, interpreting the Quranic verses by taking into account their context and the intention implicit in them. He wants to preserve and promote continuity. He hopes that Islam renewed according to his principles will convince ordinary Muslim believers that this is the religion they have inherited, the religion in which they and their ancestors have believed.

Equivalent debates

In the preceding paragraphs, I have singled out five objections raised by liberal thinkers to the renewal movement and thus to Ramadan's theology:

1. Islam is a religious ethos, not a set of rules and regulations.
2. The Quran must be studied as a human book.
3. To speak of universal values is illusory.
4. Islam's idea of truth produces authoritarianism and intolerance.
5. The authority of the *ulama* must be rejected in favour of personal freedom.

The Christian reader will notice that these five issues are also debated within the Christian community:

1. There are liberal theologians who hold that the religion of Jesus was a religious ethos fostering the love of God and neighbour, and that the institutional elements of Christianity are later constructions that obscure the original intention.
2. There are liberal scholars who hold that the Bible must be studied simply as a human book.
3. There are Christian theologians who look upon the ethics of the Gospel as altogether singular, and upon universal values as an inheritance of pagan Hellenism.
4. There are theologians who argue that the Catholic Church's claim to hold the one truth is the source of intolerance and contempt for outsiders.

5. Many Christians defend the free interpretation of the Scriptures and object to an authoritative magisterium. These five arguments are directed especially to the Catholic version of Christianity. All Christian churches defend the sacred character of the Bible, yet it is the Catholic Church that emphasizes the institutional elements of Christianity, defends the existence of universal values, claims to be the one pillar of truth, and demands obedience to its teaching authority. Progressive Catholic theologians who try to open Catholicism to pluralism and defend respectful dissent from the magisterium reread Scripture and the tradition, find approval of their positions in these Christian sources, and thus see themselves as remaining within the unbroken tradition of Catholicism.

Throughout the present study we have noticed a certain affinity between the ways Ramadan's thought and Catholic theology wrestle with the challenges of modernity. While both practise a critical openness to modernity, they resist a number of proposals made by liberal theologians of their own tradition.

With the Catholic Church, Ramadan also defends the traditional sexual teaching. Sexual intercourse is a good between a man and woman who are legally married, but in no other context. There is no room for homosexual love in Catholicism or Islam. Commentators in France have used Ramadan's defence of this prohibition as an argument that, despite some of his progressive ideas, he remains a fundamentalist. If this is the case, then the pope and the bishops must also be considered fundamentalists. Still, Ramadan has a more sympathetic understanding of the dilemma experienced by homosexual believers than any pope or bishop does. These are his words:

> I respect homosexuals and respect their choice, I cannot approve of what they do, but I respect who they are. I know, work and wrestle with men and women who are homosexual: their sexual life is their own affair. One must learn to respect the decisions of others, as long as they are not forced on them. Within the Muslim community, I am in touch with a number of homosexual men and women, some of whom suffer greatly, while others are more reconciled. They speak to me, write to me and ask my advice. I am in dialogue with them: I condemn no human being.[120]

Since Ramadan promotes so many new attitudes within Islam, it would be foolish of him to challenge the traditional sexual teaching and, in doing so, hinder the spread of the renewal movement. I find myself in a different situation in Catholicism. In 1974, in the pages of the American Catholic review *Commonweal*, I disagreed with the papal teaching and defended the moral legitimacy of homosexual love with Catholic arguments.[121] Since then, the Catholic literature on homosexuality has become extensive, at least in North America.

Ramadan differs from his liberal Muslims colleagues by the weight he attaches to every sentence of the Quran and the authentic tradition. Faced with the verse in the Sunna demanding that a man and a women not of the same family may not be left alone in a room, he first acknowledges the literal reading that has fostered the separation of men and women in Muslim societies and even in the mosques. He then searches for the universal principle in this verse that retains its validity throughout time. Implicit in this verse, he argues, is the abiding wisdom that men and women should not be left in situations that are ambiguous, that can be misunderstood or lead to abuse.[122] When faced with the words of the Prophet, "I don't shake hands with women," he will torture himself to find a universal meaning in this, instead of bracketing it altogether – as the liberals do – regarding it as a remnant of a culture that has been left behind.[123] Ramadan is a young scholar. Who knows how he will develop in the future!

This brief chapter contains an important message for readers of contemporary Muslim religious scholars. Progressive Muslim thinkers who defend a critical openness to contemporary Western society belong to two different schools of thought: they may be part of the reformist movement, *al-nahda*, which reinterprets the Islamic tradition without disrupting it, or they may be liberal religious thinkers, insisting in their method and vocabulary on the need to disrupt the tradition. Ramadan belongs to the former.

7

CONCLUDING REFLECTIONS

In this final chapter, I wish to offer a summary of Tariq Ramadan's theology based on my analysis in the preceding chapters, examine briefly the criticism raised against him, point to a certain affinity between Ramadan's theology and contemporary Catholic thought, and then present my own reaction from a Catholic perspective to the religion preached and explained by this brilliant and fascinating Muslim scholar.

Summarizing Ramadan's theology

Summoned forth by God's revelation to the Prophet, Islam is one; yet this one faith has many faces. Tariq Ramadan tells us where, in this spectrum, he locates himself. He sees himself as taking part in the renewal movement, *al-nahda*, started at the end of the nineteenth century by Jamal al-Afghani and promoted by Muslim religious thinkers from different parts of the Muslim world. Recognizing that Islam has fallen into stagnation, the reformers tried to renew Islam by an attentive rereading of the Quran and an application of human reason, following the practice of the early Islamic centuries. As a religious thinker of the reformist movement, Ramadan finds himself in disagreement with traditional Muslim orthodoxy and, even more strongly, with Muslim literalist or fundamentalist currents.

Ramadan offers a humanist interpretation of Islam. Reflecting on the Quranic teaching of God, Creator of the universe and Speaker to human beings, Ramadan arrives at a theological interpretation of human and cosmic existence. He calls this the universal message of Islam. God creates human beings by His breath; this divine breath remains with them, orients them, enables them to distinguish between good and evil, and makes them recognize their need for God. God's light shines on all men and women. The *fitra* that orients human beings toward God is in fact stamped upon the entire created order. The One God, *tahwid*, draws the entire universe into reconciliation and unity.

This Quranic message is the theological foundation for the respect that Muslims owe to every human being. Ramadan argues that this message shows that Muslims honour – or should honour – religious pluralism and personal freedom in the pursuit of religious and philosophical truth.

Muslims are grateful that in addition to the universal message, God has revealed the rituals, practices and way of life that define the *umma*, the community of believers. Because humans easily forget about God, Muslims are glad that the daily practice of *sharia* reminds them of God's goodness to them and of God's glory. While the prescriptions dealing with people's relationship to God are permanent

and unchanging, the prescriptions dealing with social relations are contextual and must be rethought in new historical
situations. The task of the *ulama*, the religious scholars, is to
extract from these prescriptions universal ethical principles
and then apply them to the concrete conditions in which
the Muslim community finds itself. This method, Ramadan
argues, reveals the flexibility of Islam. Islam is capable of
flourishing in any given society and making a contribution
to it.

Ramadan's special attention is given to Muslims living in
the West. He argues with passion that they can be faithful to
Islam, give witness to their faith and affirm their collective
identity as Muslims and, at the same time, become actively
engaged citizens working with others in the service of the
common good. He offers theological arguments that *sharia*
demands of Muslims that they obey the laws of their country: only if a particular law contradicts Islamic principles
may they express their conscientious objection. Ramadan
asks Western Muslims not to see themselves as members of
a minority, but to experience themselves as citizens in the
full sense, co-responsible with others for the well-being of
society. Because the call to citizenship is addressed to both
men and women, Muslim women experience themselves
anew in the West: they reread the Quran, emphasize the
passages that acknowledge the equality of men and women,
and wrestle against the cultural inheritance that subjugates
and humiliates women.

According to Ramadan, the experience of Western
Muslims raises questions regarding the self-understanding

of Islam that must also be faced in the East. The rulers of the so-called Muslim countries do not practise the Muslim faith. For him, *sharia* and dictatorship are incompatible. The neglect of the poor and the refusal to educate the people are violations of Muslim social ethics. According to Ramadan, today the entire world, East and West, is the place where Muslims must testify to their faith and proclaim their values as a critique of their society, even if it calls itself Muslim. Islam's call for social justice makes thinking Muslims critical of liberal capitalism, an economic system ruled by the laws of the market without respect for ethical norms. Summoned by his faith, Ramadan is deeply troubled by the massive maldistribution of wealth and power in the world. He offers an Islamic theology of universal solidarity.

At the same time, Ramadan retains certain conservative convictions. He holds that the rereading of the Quran and the enlightened application of Islamic principles to present conditions must be done by *ulama*, scholars trained in the Islamic legal tradition. He argues against several proposals made by liberal Muslim thinkers. He upholds the divine status of the Quran, he defends the authority of the *ulama*, and he honours the unbroken continuity of the Islamic tradition. He is convinced that the efforts of the renewal movement to make Islam relevant to modern democratic society are guided by fidelity to the Quran and are in keeping with the best of the Islamic tradition. He wants ordinary Muslims to be able to recognize in the reformist version of Islam the religion they have inherited.

Accusations raised against Ramadan in France

After studying Ramadan's substantial literary production, I am puzzled by the accusations raised against him in France. It seems to me that the remarks he makes in his speeches, on television and in newspapers must be understood in the light of his extensive published work. This, I think, is the only honest method. Ramadan has been accused of using a double discourse, offering one message to French society and another one to Muslim communities.[124] What disturbs me is that this accusation does not take into account the double commitment located at the heart of Ramadan's social theology. What Islam demands of Western Muslims, Ramadan argues with passion, is a double engagement to become both responsible citizens and faithful members of their religious community. Presenting this double commitment to various audiences may well demand differing emphases, depending on the context. Jewish and Christian teachers know this very well. Jews and Christians share the same double commitment to become responsible citizens and, at the same time, cultivate their collective religious identity. Many Jews and Christians, urged by their faith, take part in social movements, public debates and political projects of reform and reconstruction. What Ramadan expects of Western Muslims is no different.

As I mentioned in chapter 5, *la laïcité de l'État* – the separation of Church and state – is the national tradition of the French Republic. The state remains neutral in regard to the religions practised in the society. Ramadan repeatedly affirms that Muslim citizens of Western societies welcome *la laïcité de l'État* as long as secularity does not become a philosophy legitimating contempt for religion. Ramadan fully approves of what the bishops of Quebec call *une laïcité ouverte et tolérante* – an open and tolerant secularity.[125]

We also noted in chapter 5 that the term *le communautarisme* has taken on a pejorative meaning in France, referring to a political stance that assigns more importance to the values of a religious, ethnic or cultural community than to the universal values of freedom and equality. Communitarianism is here understood as a threat to the common good of society. To accuse Ramadan of fostering communitarianism overlooks his constant plea to Western Muslims to define themselves not as members of a minority, but as citizens working with other citizens in the service of society as a whole. Making use of sociological concepts, I have shown that Ramadan wants Muslims to constitute "a denomination," not a subculture.

Suggesting, as some critics have done, that Ramadan is a fundamentalist in disguise ignores his hermeneutical approach to the Quran and overlooks his consistent refutation of literalism. It is true, as we have seen in chapter 6, that Ramadan offers a conservative defence of the Islamic tradition against the theological liberalism of some of his colleagues, yet he does so in an intellectually sophisticated manner by rereading this classical tradition with a critical sensitivity produced by contemporary experience. A similar method is used by Catholic theologians who reread their tradition to find in it principles for guiding the good life in contemporary society.

That Ramadan is not be trusted because he is the grandson of Hassan al-Banna, the founder of the Muslim Brotherhood, seems to me a totally irrational argument.[126] For one thing, Ramadan is not a member of this community. As I mentioned in chapter 2, his extensive study of al-Banna's thought and practice has not convinced all scholars of Islam: some argue that al-Banna did not tolerate pluralism and hence should not be interpreted as a representative of the Islamic renewal. This is a debate among scholars. If Ramadan's benevolent interpretation should eventually be refuted, this would simply mean that his theological ideas were not shared by his famous grandfather. In any case, Ramadan's religious teaching must be drawn from his own published work, not from the ideas of his controversial ancestor.

Ramadan has been denounced for demanding a moratorium on the *hudud* punishments, instead of calling for their abolishment. We dealt with this misunderstanding in chapter 4.[127]

Is it true that Ramadan is anti-Semitic, as some of his critics have claimed? As I mentioned in the introduction, I made – half a century ago – a careful study of the pervasive Christian anti-Judaism and participated in the effort of the Catholic Church at the Second Vatican Council to purify its teaching, recognize the ancient covenant, honour contemporary Judaism and respect the plurality of religion. The Quran, it is generally recognized, is much less dismissive of Judaism than is the New Testament. In a theological endeavour that resembles what recent scholars have done in the Christian tradition, Ramadan rereads the Quran to show that Muslims owe respect for Judaism and for religious pluralism in general.[128]

It is because of his opposition to the military polices of the State of Israel and the occupation of Palestine that Ramadan has been accused of anti-Semitism. What made it worse is that he was once critical of some well-known Jewish authors who normally uphold universal values, yet who show partiality in their unconditional defence of Israel.[129] There was indeed a time when the critique of Israeli policies was taboo in the West. In North America, a number of university teachers lost their jobs for being critical of Israel.[130] In fact, Ramadan, invited to become a professor at Notre Dame University in the United States, was refused a work permit by the federal government – a decision influenced, it is said, by Jewish organizations that had heard of his presumed anti-Semitism. The effort to exclude the critique of Israel from the public debate assumed absurd proportions when an American university was urged not to invite Archbishop Desmond Tutu, the Nobel Prize winner, deemed anti-Semitic because of his public opposition to the occupation of Palestine.[131]

Yet this movement is coming to an end. In the U.S., an increasing number of Jews publicly criticize the politics of Israel and oppose the Occupation in particular. Best known among them is Rabbi Michael Lerner, the founded of *Tikkun* magazine and the Tikkun communities spread across many

American cities.[132] The book *Palestine: Peace Not Apartheid*,[133] by Jimmy Carter, a former President of the United States, has helped to remove the taboo from the public debate. Jewish authors have argued that an open debate in the Jewish community questioning the politics of Israel is an effective defence against anti-Semitism because it invalidates the myth of the unanimous Jewish approval of the Occupation.

In actual fact, Ramadan has repeatedly denounced the anti-Semitism that is widespread among Muslims. When they tell him that they cannot be anti-Semitic because they are themselves Semites, he replies that this discourse is a disguise: there exists hatred of Jews among Muslims.[134] To allow a political conflict to generate contempt for an entire people, Ramadan argues, is at odds with the ethics of Islam. Laura Secor, a political journalist for the Boston *Globe* who did research on Ramadan's activities in France, wrote: "I saw Ramadan exhort hundreds and even thousands of Muslims against anti-Semitism in Rennes, Lille and elsewhere. 'There is no Islamic legitimacy for antisemitism,' he told a crowd in Corbeil ... And yet, the very week of our travels, Ramadan was accused of antisemitism."[135]

Affinity between Ramadan's theology and contemporary Catholic teaching

Islam and Christianity are different religions: Muslims believe that God addresses them in the Quran, while Christians believe that God speaks to them in Jesus Christ. Still, Muslims and Christians believe in the same God. This was not widely acknowledged by Catholics in the past; it was proposed, however, by the Second Vatican Council and emphasized by Pope John Paul II.

What the present study has shown is that Catholicism and Islam also share a historical experience: both were challenged by modernity and both struggled theologically to arrive at a critical openness to modernity. We saw in chapter 1 that Catholicism repudiated modern society, condemned religious liberty and rejected the secular state and democratic pluralism. Thanks to the renewal of Catholic theology, John XXIII and Vatican Council II were able to adopt a critical openness to modernity. Catholic teaching now supports human rights, recommends democracy and respects religious pluralism, while continuing to denounce the individualism, utilitarianism and secularism promoted by modernity. We saw in the same chapter that the renewal of Catholic theology made use of three principles: i) attention to the universal message regarding the human condition, ii) attention to the changed historical circumstances, and iii) attention to the Scriptures reread with a new sensibility.

A certain analogy may be made between Catholicism and Islam: they were both embedded in a pre-modern culture and resisted the arrival of modernity, even if for different reasons. What the present study has shown is that Tariq Ramadan made a theological effort to reconsider the relation of Islam to modern society. In doing so, he made use of the same three principles: i) attention to the universal message of Islam, ii) attention to the new context in which Muslims live, and iii) attention to the Quran, reread with

a sensibility created by living in modern institutions. Ramadan's theological method allows us to speak of a certain
affinity between his critical openness to modernity and that
of contemporary Catholic thought.

This affinity is underlined by the similarity between
Ramadan's and the Church's social ethics – both supporting
social democracy, both critiquing liberal capitalism, both
demanding a more just distribution of wealth, both encouraging the social economy, and both calling for solidarity
with the poor and people at the margins. It is also worth
mentioning that Ramadan's conviction that reason reflecting
on the cosmos is capable of recognizing the Creator reveals
a metaphysical confidence that is largely absent in modern
society, yet is shared by many Catholic thinkers.

The affinity between Ramadan's theology and Catholic
thought also appears in the "conservative" defence of the
tradition that he and Catholic theologians offer to more
"liberal" believers: i.e., believers who fully embrace contemporary rationality and call for a radical break with tradition.
I have discussed this briefly in chapter 6. Ramadan speaks of
the Islamic tradition with love and respect, and, rereading
it, finds in it guidance and inspiration. The same can be said
of Catholic theologians: they keep on learning from the
Scriptures, the church fathers and the medieval thinkers. I
have often heard the parable that Protestant theologians,
troubled by the knot in a string, quickly use a knife to cut
it open, while Catholic theologians struggle, breaking their
fingernails, to unravel the knot without cutting the string.
Ramadan is also breaking his fingernails.

Theological reflections

Studying the theology of Tariq Ramadan has been a spiritual experience for me. It has also made me raise some critical questions. I find myself in dialogue with this important Muslim theologian. The following remarks mention a number of theological topics that could be the starting point for a long conversation. In this final chapter, I simply offer brief commentaries on these topics as an invitation for further reflection.

1. What impressed me in all of Ramadan's writings and, in fact, in the writings of other Muslim religious thinkers, is the constant recall of the glory of God. Human life is meaningless unless it is seen as the worship of God and the surrender to God's holy will. Here the world in which we live makes sense only if illuminated by the eternal Sun. So immense is the glory of God and so infinite God's wisdom and power that what happens on this earth, while important, is dwarfed by the Creator's infinite beauty. The smallness of personal life before the Merciful One is symbolized by the prayer of prostration: God alone deserves honour and praise. Doing good and obeying *sharia* is here a form of worship. Believers live their lives under the eternal Light.

The constant recall of God's glory had been part of the Catholic tradition before a number of contemporary experiences led many believers to other ways of focusing on God. Taking history seriously and assuming responsibility for it have made Christians hesitate to think of God as residing in another realm. They prefer to think of God as present in history, forgiving, summoning and empowering people to create a just and friendly world. Moreover, the Holocaust and other horrors of the 20th and 21st centuries have made it impossible for many believers to think of God as the heavenly ruler of human history. Refusing to believe that there is room for these massive crimes in God's providence, many Christians prefer to think of God in solidarity with Christ crucified and with all the victims of history, opting for powerlessness (*kenosis*) out of love. In these experiences, God is thought of as present in history —not identified with history nor imprisoned in it, but present in transcendent freedom. This is the spirituality in which I have found myself for many decades.

Encountering in Ramadan's writings the constant recall of God's glory has been a religious experience for me. I now find that the *Gloria in excelsis Deo* of the Eucharistic liturgy speaks to me in a new way. With different ears I now hear *Laudamus te, benedicamus te, adoramus te, glorificamus te, gratias agimus tibi propter magnam gloriam tuam.* I conclude that dialogue with a non-Christian religion may lead us to appropriate our own tradition in a new way.

2. What I did not find in Ramadan's theology is the anguish over the omnipresence of evil that Christians refer to as original sin. As a Catholic in the Augustinian tradition, I am deeply troubled by the injustice, the inequality, the domination, the exploitation and the scandalous maldistribution of wealth and power in the world, which causes endless suffering and distorts the consciousness of all, including the victims. Children born into this world inherit

these wounds. This sinful condition has a tragic character: while we can be forgiven, we can never fully escape the consequences of the sinful condition. I am 85 years old and in reasonably good health, while in vast regions of the world, people's longevity is 50 years and declining. Why, I ask, do I get over 35 years more than they do? The answer is simple: I live in a wealthy society and thus participate in the criminally unjust system that divides humanity into rich and poor. Yet the dominant culture in the West makes the sin of the world almost invisible: to detect it, to become seeing, one must be touched by the Spirit.

Reading Ramadan gives me the impression that he shares this awareness and these sentiments, but I do not see them articulated in theological terms.

3. Trusting the divine blessings, Tariq Ramadan approaches the challenges of human existence with confidence. He shares this hopeful attitude with other Sunni Muslim thinkers. In his major study of Islam, Hans Küng has argued that Islam is a religion of success. The Prophet succeeded in leading the idolatrous Arabian tribes into the community of faith in the one true God. By contrast, the earthly mission of Jesus was a failure. He was born into the Jewish society colonized by the Roman Empire that promoted cultural values at odds with the faith of Israel and imposed its harsh rule with the help of the Jewish elites loyal to Caesar – the vassal kings and the high priests. In this situation, Jesus announced the coming of God's reign, a life in community based on principles in contradiction with the Empire, a mission that made him enemies and led

to his crucifixion. Only at his resurrection did the disciples
discover who he really was. It is not success, but defeat and
resurrection – the paschal mystery – that guides Christians
in their perception of what goes on in the world.

Shiite Muslims have a greater sense of the tragic dimension in human life than do Sunni Muslims. Shiites remember the martyrdom of Hussein, Ali's son, killed with his
followers in the year 680 in an uprising against Muawiya,
the caliph regarded by them as illegitimate. To this day,
Shiite Muslims sorrow over Hussein's violent death, the
symbol of failed resistance to tyranny. Their faith in God's
blessings does not prevent them from lamenting the human
condition.

4. A significant difference exists between the Islamic
and Christian understandings of law, even in Ramadan's
reformist interpretation. In Islam, laws are seen in the most
positive light. Muslims are grateful for the laws God has
given them. Muslims will interpret them, adjusting them to
the historical context, yet once reformulated, they oblige.
Reflecting on the laws, Muslim ethics ponders what is
recommended, what is permitted, what is discouraged and
what is forbidden.

By contrast, the New Testament problematizes the law,
even the Torah, the Law given by God. Jesus dispenses his
disciples from the law of the Sabbath by appealing to a
higher obligation: the love of neighbour (Mt 12, Mk 2, Lk
6). While laws play an important role in the life of society,
they may be disregarded under certain conditions. "The
Sabbath was made for man, not man for the Sabbath" (Mk

2:27). Already the Hebrew Scriptures suggest that laws, even divinely given laws, burden the soul and lead to conformist behaviour. That is why Jeremiah prophesies that in the messianic days, the laws will be sunk into the human heart, and humans will praise God and do good spontaneously. "This is the covenant I shall make with the House of Israel when those days have come ... I shall plant my law within them, writing it on their hearts" (Jer. 31:33). While Jesus followed the Torah, albeit with great freedom, the Apostle Paul dispenses Christians from the Law, using a radical rhetoric that reveals the problematic character of laws. Jesus had been condemned as a transgressor of religious and secular laws. "Christ redeemed us from the curse of the law by being cursed for our sake since Scripture says, 'Anyone hanged is accursed'" (Gal. 3:13). When the Apostle declares that Christians "no longer live under the law, but under grace" (Rom. 6:14), he refers not only to the Torah but to all laws. At best, laws constitute a pedagogy for people who start living the moral life, yet since laws create general obligations, they disregard the particular case and are therefore capable of condemning the innocent. This happened to Jesus. With his resurrection, the Apostle declares, the messianic days have come; God imprints the law on the hearts of his people and guides the moral life of believers by the impulse of grace. Because God's love is poured into their hearts, men and women of faith will be able to lead a life of love. Admittedly, this enthusiastic teaching is not the last word of the Apostle. He later finds himself obliged to introduce laws into the Christian communities.

Yet the problematizing of the law in the New Testament has not been without influence upon Christian life and theology, especially in the Protestant tradition. Yet even the Catholic tradition recognized the virtue of *epikeia*, or equity. Here is the famous text from St. Thomas's *Summa theologica* II-II, question 120, art. 1:

> Since human actions, with which laws are concerned, are composed of contingent singulars and are innumerable in their diversity, it was not possible to lay down rules of law that would apply to every single case. Legislators in framing laws attend to what commonly happens: although if the law be applied to certain cases it will frustrate the equality of justice and be injurious to the common good which the law has in view. ... [There are] cases where it is bad to follow the law, and it is good to set aside the letter of the law and to follow the dictates of justice and the common good ... Therefore it is evident that "epikeia" is a virtue.

5. Tariq Ramadan is in dialogue with modernity. Since modern society has been produced by two revolutionary institutions, political democracy and capitalist industrialization, and is therefore subject to never-ending internal tensions, modern society demands a carefully nuanced response. On the basis of his Muslim faith, Ramadan welcomes democratic freedoms and political co-responsibility; at the same time he laments the emancipation of science, technology and the economy from the constraint of an ethical framework. He actually looks for allies in modern society who demand the restoration of ethics to provide normative guidance for techno-scientific developments and the production, exchange and consumption of goods.

In the encyclical *Spe salvi* (2008), on Christian hope, Pope Benedict XVI also recognizes that modernity has produced its own critique and that Christians guided by their faith should be in dialogue with these critics. Here is an interesting paragraph:

> A self-critique of modernity is needed in dialogue with Christianity and its concept of hope. In this dialogue Christians too, in the context of their knowledge and experience, must learn anew in what their hope truly consists, what they have to offer to the world and what they cannot offer. Flowing into this self-critique of the modern age there also has to be a self-critique of Christianity, which must constantly renew its self-understanding, setting out from its roots." (#22)

What Benedict XVI does not say is that secular thinkers reflecting critically on modernity should also be in dialogue with Islam and the other world religions.

Reading Tariq Ramadan's writings and following the development of Catholic social thought, I am persuaded that the time has come for a dialogue of Muslims and Christians with secular thinkers intent on protecting the *humanum* in society and the world at large. The dialogue of Jürgen Habermas and Joseph Ratzinger held in Munich in 2004, prior to Ratzinger's elevation to the papacy, was a boundary-crossing event that caught the attention of intellectuals and provided a model to be followed in other contexts, with other participants.[136] Dialogue among believers of different religions is, on the whole, much easier than dialogue between believers and non-believers, since the latter tend to assign faith in spiritual transcendence to the emotions and hence think of theology as an exercise in wishful thinking. Yet since the fate of humanity depends on universal human cooperation, the time for religious-secular dialogue has come.

Appendix

The Ten Commandments for Peace

1. We commit ourselves to proclaiming our firm conviction that violence and terrorism are incompatible with the authentic spirit of religion, and, as we condemn every recourse to violence and war in the name of God or of religion, we commit ourselves to doing everything possible to eliminate the root causes of terrorism.

2. We commit ourselves to educating people to mutual respect and esteem, in order to help bring about a peaceful and fraternal coexistence between people of different ethnic groups, cultures and religions.

3. We commit ourselves to fostering the culture of dialogue, so that there will be an increase of understanding and mutual trust between individuals and among peoples, for these are the premise of authentic peace.

4. We commit ourselves to defending the right of everyone to live a decent life in accordance with their own cultural identity, and to form freely a family of his own.

5. We commit ourselves to frank and patient dialogue, refusing to consider our differences as an insurmountable barrier, but recognizing instead that to encounter the diversity of others can become an opportunity for greater reciprocal understanding.

6. We commit ourselves to forgiving one another for past and present errors and prejudices, and to supporting one another in a common effort both to overcome selfishness and arrogance, hatred and violence, and to learn from the past that peace without justice is no true peace.

7. We commit ourselves to taking the side of the poor and the helpless, to speaking out for those who have no voice and to working effectively to change these situations, out of the conviction that no one can be happy alone.

8. We commit ourselves to taking up the cry of those who refuse to be resigned to violence and evil, and we desire to make every effort possible to offer the men and women of our time real hope for justice and peace.

9. We commit ourselves to encouraging all efforts to promote friendship between peoples, for we are convinced that, in the absence of solidarity and understanding between peoples, technological progress exposes the world to a growing risk of destruction and death.

10. We commit ourselves to urging leaders of nations to make every effort to create and consolidate, on the national and international levels, a world of solidarity and peace based on justice.

This Decalogue of Assisi for Peace is part of a letter sent by Pope John Paul II "to all heads of states and governments" on March 4, 2002.

Notes

1   Tariq Ramadan, *Être musulman européen*, translation from the English by Claude Dubbak (Lyon: Éd. Tawhid, 1999); *Aux sources du renouveau musulman* (Paris: Bayard Éditions, 1998); *Les musulmans d'Occident ou l'avenir de l'Islam* (Paris : Sindbad/Actes Sud, 2003).

2   *Nostra aetate*, 3, in Walter Abbot, ed., *The Documents of Vatican II* (New York: Herder, 1966), 663.

3   Tariq Ramadan, *To Be a European Muslim* (Leicester, UK: The Islamic Foundation, 1999) and *Western Muslims and the Future of Islam* (New York: Oxford University Press, 2004).

4   Caroline Fourest, *Frère Tariq* (Paris: Grasset, 2004); Lionel Favrot, *Tariq Ramadan dévoilé* (Lion: Lion Mag, 2004); Paul Landau, *Le sabre et le Coran: Tariq Ramadan et les frères musulmans à la conquête de l'Europe* (Paris: Édition du Rocher, 2005).

5   Aziz Zemouri, *Faut-il faire taire Tariq Ramadan?* (Paris: l'Archipel, 2005).

6   Zemouri also analyzes why le père Christian Delorme withdrew his support of Ramadan: the contentious issue was related not to Ramadan's teaching, but to his organizational involvement: Zemouri, *Faut-il faire taire Tariq Ramadan?* 16, 31–33, 146–47.

7   Ian Hamel, *La vérité sur Tariq Ramadan* (Lausanne/Paris: Favre, 2007).

8   Recently, President Sarkozy has proposed an interpretation of *la laïcité* that respects religious communties. Henri Tincq, "Sarkozy et Dieu," *Le Monde*, Feb. 14, 2008.

9   American Civil Liberties Union, 1/24/2006: www.aclu.org/safefree/general/23588res20060124.html (accessed February 1, 2008).

10 In Canada, Ramadan has been consulted by the Minister of Foreign Affairs, the Institute for Research and Public Policy (IRRP) and the Ottawa Police Department.

11 "Christians joyfully recognize the religious values we have in common with Islam. Today I would like to repeat what I said to young Muslims some years ago in Casablanca: 'We believe in the same God, the one God, the living God, the God who created the world and brings his creatures to their perfection.'" John Paul II, general audience, May 5, 1999: his address at Casablanca occurred on August 19, 1985.

12 Hans Küng, *Der Islam: Geschichte, Gegenwart, Zukunft* (München: Piper, 2006).

13 http://www.americancatholiclawyers.org/encyclical%20-%20notre%20charge.htm (accessed February 1, 2008).

14 Gregory Baum, *Religion and Alienation* (Ottawa: Novalis, 2007).

15 http://www.anu.edu.au/polsci/marx/classics/manifesto.html (accessed February 1, 2008).

16 David Martin, *A General Theory of Secularisation* (Oxford: Blackwell, 1978).

17   Hakan Yavuz, ed. *Turkish Islam and the Secular State: The Gülen Movement* (Syracuse, NY: Syracuse University Press, 2003).

18   Paul Blanshard, *American Freedom and Catholic Power* (Boston: Beacon Press, 1949).

19   Samuel Huntington, *The Clash of Civilizations and the Remaking of World Order* (New York: Simon & Schuster, 1996).

20   See the article "thèse et hypothèse" in the encyclopedia *Catholicisme* (Paris: Letouzey et Ané) vol. 14, 1996, 1149–51.

21   Jacques Maritain, *Antimoderne* (Paris: Desclée de Brouwer, 1922).

22   Jacques Maritain, *Primauté du spirituel* (Paris: Plon, 1927).

23   Maritain, *Primauté du spirituel*, 106.

24   Jacques Maritain, *Du régime temporel et de la liberté* (Paris: Desclée de Brouwer, 1933).

25   Jacques Maritain, *Christianisme et démocratie* (New York: Éditions de la Maison Française, 1943).

26   *Pacem in terris*, no. 3.

27   *Pacem in terris*, no. 10.

28   *Pacem in terris*, no. 8.

29   Giuseppe Alberigo, ed., *History of Vatican II*, vol. iv (Maryknoll, NY: Orbis, 2003), 96–134, 388–405.

30   Paul Valadier, *Maritain à contre-temps* (Paris: Desclée de Brouwer, 2007), 116.

31   See Appendix.

32   Gregory Baum, *The Priority of Labour: A Commentary on "Laborem exercens"* (New York: Paulist Press, 1982); *Theology and Society* (New York: Paulist Press, 1987); "The Priority of Labour over Capital: Pope John Paul II's Social Teaching," in *Signs of the Times* (Ottawa: Novalis, 2007), 121–44.

33   Zemouri, *Faut-il faire taire Tariq Ramadan?* 227–44.

34   *Populorum Progressio*, no. 30.

35   Abdel Haleem, "Introduction," *The Quran* (New York: Oxford University Press, 2006), xviii. See also chapter 6.

36   Tariq Ramadan, *In the Footsteps of the Prophet: Lessons from the Life of Mohammad* (New York: Oxford University Press, 2007).

37   Ramadan, *To Be a European Muslim*, 28.

38   Tariq Ramadan, *Islam, le face à face des civilisations* (Paris: Tawhid, 2001), 35.

39   Ramadan, *To Be a European Muslim*, 32.

40   Ramadan, *To Be a European Muslim*, 31–43.

41   See Küng, *Der Islam*, 346–69.

42   In his book, Hans Küng offers a comparative study of Al-Gazzali and St. Thomas Aquinas. Küng, *Der Islam*, 436–46.

43   Ramadan, *To Be a European Muslim*, 38.

44   Ramadan, *Aux sources du renouveau musulman*, 1998.

45   Xavier Ternisien, *Les frères musulmans* (Paris: Fayyard, 2005) offers an interpretation of the Brotherhood that is close to Ramadan's.

46   Ramadan, *Western Muslims and the Future of Islam*, 26.

47   Ramadan, *To Be a European Muslim*, 239–45; *Western Muslims and the Future of Islam*, 24–30.

48   Hakan Yavuz, ed., *Turkish Islam and the Secular State* (Syracuse, NY: Syracuse University Press, 2003); Gregory Baum, "Fethullah Gülen: Theism and Modernity," *The Ecumenist*, 45 (Winter 2008), 10–15.

49   Ramadan, *To Be a European Muslim*, 243.

50   Ramadan, *Western Muslims and the Future of Islam*, 11–24.

51   Ramadan, *Western Muslims and the Future of Islam*, 11–12.

52   Ramadan, *Western Muslims and the Future of Islam*, 12 (Quran 24:41).

53   Ramadan, *Western Muslims and the Future of Islam*, 16.

54   Ramadan, *Western Muslims and the Future of Islam*, 16 (Quran 30:30).

55   Ramadan, *Western Muslims and the Future of Islam*, 18 (Quran 6:165).

56   Mohamed Talbi, *Universalité du coran* (Arles: Actes Sud, 2002), 52.

57   See especially *Gaudium et spes*, 22, *Nostra aetate*, 2, also Gregory Baum, *Amazing Church: A Catholic Theologian Remembers a Half-Century of Change* (Ottawa: Novalis, 2005), 35–44.

58   Ramadan, *Western Muslims and the Future of Islam*, 79.

59   "Fanaticism, being violent and unreasoning devotion, is incompatible with Islam. However deep it is, Muslim devotion depends on knowledge and reasoning. For the deeper and firmer a Muslim's belief in and devotion to Islam … the further from fanaticism a Muslim by virtue of Islam being 'the middle way' based on peace, balance, justice and moderation." Quoted in Robert Hunt et al., eds., *Muslim Citizens of the Globalized World* (Somerset, NJ: The Light, 2006), 18.

60   Ahmer Kuru, "Fethullah Gülen's Search for a Middle Way," in Yavuz, ed., *Turkish Islam and the Secular State*, 115–30.

61   See pages 107–08 below.

62   In his famous speech at the University of Regensburg in 2006, Pope Benedict XVI proposed that the God of Islam is a God of absolute freedom who decides what is good and what is bad arbitrarily, while, by contrast, the freedom of the Christian God is guided by divine intelligence and hence respects the order created by Him. Muslim scholars corrected the Pope's interpretation. If the Pope had read Ramadan, he would not have made his controversial proposal. Gregory Baum, *Signs of the Times* (Ottawa: Novalis, 2007), 132–34; "Open Letter to His Holiness Benedict XVI," *The Ecumenist*, 43 (fall 2006), 1–6.

63   Richard Foltz et al., eds., *Islam and Ecology* (Cambridge, MA: Harvard University Press, 2003).

64   Already in 1944, the political economist Karl Polanyi had published his classic study *The Great Transformation*, in which he analyzed the devastating impact of the unregulated market system on the natural environment – an aspect that the socialist critics of capitalism had overlooked.

65   *Science*, 155 (1967), 1203–07.

66   Seyyed Hossein Nasr, *The Encounter of Man and Nature: The Spiritual Crisis of Modern Man* (London: Allen & Unwin, 1968).

67   Ali Ünal et al., eds., *Fethullah Gülen: Advocate of Dialogue* (Fairfax, VA: The Fountain, 2000), 75–81.

68   Elisabeth Özdalga, "Following in the Footsteps of Fethullah Gülen," in Yavuz, ed. *Turkish Islam and the Secular State*, 85–114.

69   http://atos.ouvaton.org/article.php3?id_article=49 (accessed August 28, 2008).

70   Haleen, "Introduction," *The Quran*, xviii.

71   Ramadan, *Western Muslims and the Future of Islam*, 26.

72   Ramadan, *To Be a European Muslim*, 191, 241; *Western Muslims*, 26, 37–38, 80.

73   Ramadan, *Islam, le face à face des civilisations*, 35.

74   *Catechism of the Catholic Church* (Vatican: Libreria Editrice Vaticana, 2000), no. 110.

75   This verse is interpreted in Haleen, "Introduction," *The Quran*, xxii.

76   *Encyclopedia of the Orient*, "Muslim iconoclasm" (http://i-cias.com/e.o/mus_iconoclasm.htm) accessed February 1, 2008.

77   On the difficult topic of Islam and art, see Ramadan, *To Be a European Muslim*, 201–06.

78   Ramadan, *Aux sources du renouveau musulman*, 124.

79   Farid Esack, *Coran, mode d'emploi* (Paris: Albin Michel, 2004), 49–50.

80   Ramadan, *To Be a European Muslim*, 63.

81   Ramadan, *To Be a European Muslim*, 64.

82   CBC News, "Sharia Law in Ontario", May 26, 2005. www.cbc.ca/news/background/islam/shariah-law.html (accessed February 1, 2008).

83   Tariq Ramadan, "An International Call for a Moratorium of Corporal Punishments," May 30, 2005. www.tariqramadan.com/call.php3?id_article=264&lang=en (accessed February 1, 2008).

84   Huntington, *The Clash of Civilisations and the Remaking of World Order*.

85   Ramadan, *Western Muslims and the Future of Islam*, 73–77.

86   Ramadan, *To Be a European Muslim*, 142.

87   Ramadan, *To Be a European Muslim*, 132–34.

88   Ramadan, *To Be a European Muslim*, 161–62.

89   Ramadan, *To Be a European Muslim*, 168.

90   Ramadan, *To Be a European Muslim*, 189.

91   Ramadan, *To Be a European Muslim*, 190–95.

92   Ramadan, *Western Muslims and the Future of Islam*, 53.

93   Gregory Baum, "The Church in a North American Perspective," in Gerard Mannion, ed., *The Routledge Companion of the Christian Church* (New York; Routledge 2008), 306–25, 327–30.

94   *Dictionnaire d'éthique et de philosophie morale*, Monique Canto-Sperber, dir. (Paris: Presses Universitaire de France, 1996), 280–87.

95   Ramadan, *Western Muslims and the Future of Islam*, 159.

96   Ramadan, *Western Muslims and the Future of Islam*, 159.

97   On this law, see www.herodote.net/histoire/evenement.php?jour=19051209 (accessed February 1, 2008).

98   Ramadan, *Western Muslims and the Future of Islam*, 144–99; Ramadan, *Islam, le face à face des civisilations*, 58–62, 148–62.

99   *The Catechism of the Catholic Church*, no. 2425.

100 *Populorum progressio*, no. 26.

101 Ramadan, *Western Muslims and the Future of Islam*, 199.

102 *Populorum progressio*, no. 30.

103 Ramadan, *Islam, le face à face des civilisations*, 186–95.

104 Zemouri, *Faut-il faire taire Tariq Ramadan?* 227–44.

105 Ramadan, *Western Muslims and the Future of Islam*, 138.

106 Lene Rasmussen, "Muslim women and intellectuals in 20th-century Egyptian debate," The fourth Nordic Conference on Middle Eastern Studies, Oslo, Aug. 13–16, 1998, www.hf.uib.no/smi/pao/kofoed.html (accessed February 1, 2008); Osire Glacier, "Le féminisme arabe," *Relations*, septembre 2007, 30–32.

107 *American Muslim*, January/February 2006, 60.

108 *Les débats du Nouvel Observateur: Ils veulent réformer l'islam*, 4–10 juillet 2002.

109 Ramadan, *Western Muslims and the Future of Islam*, 139–40.

110 H. Denzinger, ed., *Enchiridion Symbolorum* (Freiburg: Herder, 1963), 342, no. 1351.

111 *Nostra aetate*, no. 2. Also "Since Christ died for all [humans], and since the ultimate vocation of [humans] is in fact one, and divine, we ought to believe that the Holy Spirit in a manner known only to God offers to every [human being] the possibility of being associated with this paschal mystery" (*Gaudium et spes*, no. 22).

112 Ramadan, *Western Muslims and the Future of Islam*, 202.

113 *Journal of Ecumenical Studies*, 39 (Winter–Spring 2002), 26.

114 Ramadan, *Western Muslims and the Future of Islam*, 210.

115 Farish Noor interviewed six of the participants of the Conference – Abdullah An-Naim, Abdolkarim Soroush, Ebrahim Moosa, Ansghar Engineer, Nurcholish Madjid and Chandra Muzaffar – producing an entire book available on the ISIM website: www.isim.nl/files/paper_noor.pdf (accessed August 27, 2008).

116 The report is available on the ISIM website: www.isim.nl/files/muslim_intellectuals_report.doc (accessed August 27, 2008).

117 This objection was raised by Abdolkarim Soroush, Abdelmajid Charfi, Abu Zaid, and Ebrahim Moosa.

118 World Conference of Religions for Peace, www.religionsforpeace.org (accessed February 1, 2008).

119 On the *hudud* punishments, see chapter 4, p. 101–04.

120 Zemouri, *Faut-il faire taire Tariq Ramadan?* 180.

121 *Commonweal*, 99 (1974), 479–82.

122 Zemouri, *Faut-il faire taire Tariq Ramadan?* 203–04.

123   Zemouri, *Faut-il faire taire Tariq Ramadan?* 214–15.
124   Ramadan replies to this accusation in the article "Quel double discourse? Quel débat?" in *Libération*, 25. Nov. 2003, reprinted in Zemouri, *Faut-il faire taire Tariq Ramadan?* 359–62. Zemouri questions Ramadan on this issue, 65–93.
125   Testimony of the Quebec bishops before la Commission Bouchard-Taylor; see *Le Devoir*, 13 déc. 2007, A5.
126   For Ramadan's response to this suspicion, see Zemouri, 95–132.
127   See pages 101–04.
128   See pages 134–38.
129   See Ramadan's article "Critique des (nouveaux) intellectuels communautaristes" reprinted in Zemouri, 323–26. The subsequent public debate in France provoked Edgar Morin to write the article "Antisémitisme, anti-judaïsme, anti-israëlisme," *Le Monde*, Feb. 19, 2004, to show the injustice of accusing of anti-Semitism all critics of the Israeli occupation of Palestine. The article was widely appreciated in France and reprinted in translation in the United States.
130   Judy Haiven, "Academic Freedom for Some," *Outlook: Canada's Progressive Jewish Magazine*, 46 (Jan./Feb. 2008), 15.
131   www.alternet.org/audits/64314/ (accessed February 1, 2008).
132   www.tikkun.org/ (accessed February 1, 2008).
133   Jimmy Carter, *Palestine: Peace Not Apartheid* (New York: Simon & Schuster, 2006).
134   See Ramadan's article « Existe-til un antisémitisme islamique?" in *Le Monde*, Dec. 23, 2001, reprinted in Zemouri, *Faut-il faire taire Tariq Ramadan?* 327–29.
135   Laura Secor, "Tariq Ramadan, a Reformer to his Admirers, a Dangerous Theocrat to his Detractors," *The Boston Globe*, Nov. 30, 2003, www.encyclopedia.com/doc/1P2-7814820.html (accessed February 1, 2008).
136   www.kath-akademie-bayern.de/contentserv/www.katholische.de/index.php?StoryID=194 (accessed February 1, 2008).